KU-794-804

CALL THE MIDWIFE

A LABOUR OF LOVE

Also by Stephen McGann

Flesh and Blood:
A History of My Family in Seven Maladies

Doctor Turner's Casebook

CALL THE MIDWIFE

A LABOUR OF LOVE

Ten years of life, love and laughter

STEPHEN McGANN

with behind-the-scenes
interviews by **Henrietta Bredin**

WEIDENFELD & NICOLSON

First published in Great Britain in 2021 by Weidenfeld & Nicolson
an imprint of The Orion Publishing Group Ltd
Carmelite House, 50 Victoria Embankment
London EC4Y 0DZ

An Hachette UK Company

1 3 5 7 9 10 8 6 4 2

Photographers: Laurence Cendrowicz, Jonathan Ford, Nicky Johnston, Des Willie

Call the Midwife
A Neal Street Production for the BBC

A CIP catalogue record for this book is
available from the British Library.

ISBN (Hardback) 978 1 4746 2449 7
ISBN (eBook) 978 1 4746 2450 3

Editorial: Maddy Price, Georgia Goodall
Design: Clare Sivell
Printed and Bound in Italy by Printer Trento

www.weidenfeldandnicolson.co.uk
www.orionbooks.co.uk

TO THE REAL MIDWIVES AND
NURSES, PAST AND PRESENT,
HERE AND EVERYWHERE

CONTENTS

CALL THE MIDWIFE

A LABOUR OF LOVE

INTRODUCTION

Stephen McGann

Dr Turner

———

I'm on a street in west London. It's January 2012. I press the mobile phone harder to my ear to cut out the sound of traffic and the chattering of passing students. It's Heidi – my partner, and the writer of *Call the Midwife*. She excitedly repeats the overnight viewing figure for the second episode of Series One. Her voice is clear but it takes a moment to comprehend what she's saying. The figure she's telling me is big. Really big. Half a million up on last week's stupidly big figure. After the first episode, figures are supposed to go down, not up. Everybody knows that . . .

'The BBC have been in touch. They want to recommission it straight away!'

The call ends and I stand on the kerb, letting the people and the traffic pass me by. One of those sweet moments when life shifts a gear and the grey sky becomes flecked with new colour. I'm elated. For her. For it. For all of us. Our little show. The drama we'd spent the previous summer making in a disused seminary in north London. Our brave, fierce, gentle, tough little show. *Call the Midwife* is a hit. A great big hit. And no one saw it coming.

Ten years is a strange length of time – long enough for memories to gain a tinge of fog but still near enough to recall those moments of sharp emotion, or the thrill of a sudden life change. *Call the Midwife* was never a 'big' drama. Not in its initial planning, or in its moving execution, or even in its subsequent ecstatic reception. One of the things I love about *Call the Midwife* is that it's a small, intimate drama on the inside but one that appears much bigger when viewed from the outside. A sort of reverse of *Doctor Who*'s Tardis. It was never the kind of glossy period production that presumed it would get the public's attention. Far from it. In a way, it's more like the courageous but unassuming women it portrays. Its virtue doesn't lie in a cavalier swagger or lavish self-confidence. It comes from something far more enduring. Quiet compassion. An unshakeable humanity. Absolute sincerity. An ability to reach out of the TV screen and grasp the hearts and minds of the viewers, week in, week out.

That's why I think it's so easy to underestimate the visceral impact *Call the Midwife* has on its audience. We live in a world of competing noise and bids for our attention. The constant cackle of style over substance. A cacophony of frantic wants and needs and desires. Compassion and sincerity, by contrast, don't tend to shout because the most meaningful and moving moments in all our lives exist in that breath-held silence between louder but less important things. That place where the stuff of life really happens. This is at the quiet heart of all good drama. The birthing room where *Call the Midwife* does all of its gentle work.

It's funny to recall a time, all those years back, when I'd never heard the phrase 'Call the Midwife'. The bestselling book by Jennifer Worth had somehow passed me by but our wonderful producer, Pippa Harris, had sent Heidi a copy to read with a view to adapting it for television. This, in itself, wasn't noteworthy. Writers of historical drama like Heidi are frequently sent books to consider – and most of them end up adding to the growing mountain of night-time reading we stack by our bedside. Heidi reads voraciously and fast, and doesn't waste time on something that doesn't grab her – so I'm accustomed to seeing her pick up and discard books with the frequency of a French courtesan dispensing with unprofitable suitors. But this time it was different. She became engrossed. I absent-mindedly referred to it as 'that midwife one'. If I asked her an idle question while she was reading, it would take her several seconds to reply. Occasionally, I'd hear her gasp under her breath or let out a small sigh. Eventually, she broke her silence with a single understatement that still has me laughing a decade on.

'You know, I think I might be able to do something with this . . .'

She was right of course. She *was* able to 'do something' with *Call the Midwife*. And over the last decade, the results have been seen on televisions all over the world. Yet the modesty in that statement stays with me because it typifies her approach to the subject matter and what I think sets *Call the Midwife* apart from other TV dramas. Heidi had immediately understood the dramatic power of Jennifer Worth's world and seen how it might be transposed to television. But this transposition wasn't a cynical formula; instead, it would empathise fully with those humans it portrayed.

The supposed 'woman's world' of childbirth had spent too many years in the shadows of TV drama, reduced to a few panting seconds in the service of more masculine plotlines. The medical women in Jennifer's stories were hardened by experience and yet remained devoted to the care of those who endured lives of invisibility, indifference, pain and shame with phenomenal stoicism. If the fundamental human experience of childbirth as a springboard for wider life drama was ever going to get the attention it deserved, then it would be by telling their unheard stories with respect and sincerity. Showing their faith, their frailties, their grief and their joy without judgement or a cynical tongue in a cheek.

I think *Call the Midwife* makes people cry every week because it makes Heidi cry when she writes it. It makes us actors cry when we play it. *Call the Midwife* is celebrating its tenth anniversary because those of us involved with it absolutely mean what we do. We're as much members of the audience for these stories as our viewers. Because, ultimately, these stories are about all of us. What we all have in common and how we might care a bit better for each other.

If that isn't worth ten years of labour, then I don't know what is.

SERIES ONE

1957

EPISODE ONE

Unworldly new midwife Jenny Lee arrives at Nonnatus House to join midwives Trixie Franklin and Cynthia Miller, and nuns Sister Julienne, Sister Evangelina, Sister Bernadette and Sister Monica Joan in their community work. She has trouble adjusting to her new job and the harsh East End environment but when she handles Spanish mum Conchita Warren's traumatic birth alone, she knows she's made the right choice.

EPISODE TWO

Friendly but accident-prone Camilla Fortescue-Cholmeley-Browne, nicknamed Chummy, arrives with a crash, bang and bicycle wobble, much to Sister Evangelina's frustration. Jenny takes care of young Irish prostitute and mum-to-be Mary – but finds that the world can be cruel to a condemned woman in need of a second chance.

EPISODE THREE

Trixie and Cynthia look after Winnie Lawson, a woman in her forties who is upset at getting pregnant, despite her husband Ted's excitement. They understand her distress when she eventually gives birth to a mixed-race child. When Jenny is assigned old soldier Joe Collett to care for, she is disgusted by his bug-infested living conditions but comes to admire the man beneath the grime and hatches a plan to honour him.

EPISODE FOUR

There is shock when Shirley Redmond's new baby is snatched from its pram and the entire community is mobilised to recover the infant. When the perpetrator is discovered to be traumatised Mary from episode two, Jenny intervenes to protect both child and thief. Meanwhile, Cynthia witnesses the pain and resilience of love as headmaster David Jones loses his beloved musician wife Margaret to eclampsia.

EPISODE FIVE

When Nonnatus House cleaner Peggy's brother Frank develops cancer, Jenny and the nuns are glad to look after him. But as the Nonnatuns learn of the siblings' harsh workhouse upbringing they discover that their relationship is more intimate than anyone expected. Meanwhile, Fred Buckle, the caretaker, has a new money-making scheme: making a fortune in bacon from a new pig called Evie. But when Evie is discovered to be pregnant, Fred's plans are scuppered and the team's midwifery skills are given a whole new twist.

EPISODE SIX

Sister Monica Joan has Nonnatus House deeply concerned when she catches pneumonia after roaming the streets. But when she is later arrested for theft and put on trial, the team are worried that her roaming days may be over for good. Meanwhile, Chummy's snobbish mother visits the convent to pour cold water on her daughter's relationship with the lowly PC Noakes. Chummy reluctantly ends their relationship but the other midwives bring about a change of heart and the episode concludes with the couple's wedding.

CHRISTMAS 1957

An abandoned baby is discovered on the steps of the convent. The whole team rallies round to provide food and clothing, and a search is organised to trace his mother. Chummy sets herself the task of mounting a children's nativity play, while Jenny and Dr Turner become involved in the distressing case of Mrs Jenkins – an elderly vagrant with a cruel workhouse past, and the unbearable pain of a mother's unresolved loss.

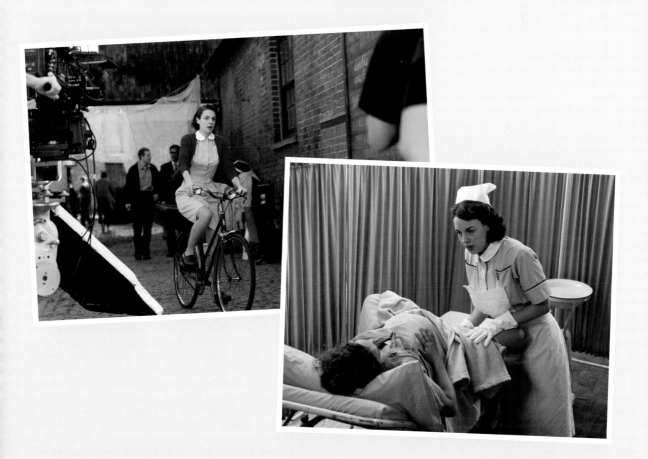

BIRTH OF A LEGEND

Stephen McGann

Dr Turner

'*Call the Midwife*? That's just about babies being born, isn't it?'

I still get that sometimes from members of the public who've never watched the programme. Those who have know that *Call the Midwife* is about a great deal more than that! But the remark still makes me smile – the assumption that being the first drama to represent the universal human experience of childbirth on pre-watershed television is somehow an achievement so trivial it deserves the word 'just' in front of it!

In truth, there was no 'just' about it. When we first gathered to make Series One in early 2011, a major task for the production team was how to create the joy, pain and breath-held drama of childbirth in a way that fully respected medical practice and female biology, and yet was watchable for a family audience. Until then, childbirth on screen tended to be a technical afterthought: a few seconds of light panting in full make-up before a three-month-old baby pops out. This careless dismissal of such a profound process would regularly drive real midwives crazy. But not this time. We were going into that closed world of the birthing room and wanted to do justice to an event that literally every human being has experienced. As Dr Turner, I was fortunate to play a small part in those early scenes – and so witnessed at first-hand the incredible combination of teamwork and expertise that achieved them.

The major birth in episode one was a hell of a way to start. Exclusively Spanish-speaking Conchita Warren (played brilliantly by Carolina Valdés), mother of twenty-four (!) children. A premature delivery with life-threatening complications. Jessica Raine's first major birth challenge as midwife Jenny Lee. Those scenes would probably define the success or failure of our entire series. No pressure, then!

We were lucky to possess a secret weapon in the form of our midwifery advisor and real-life midwife, Terri Coates. Terri had years of clinical experience and was determined to see her job represented with dignity and accuracy at last. Yet all that expertise would be worthless if Terri wasn't also a part of the wider dramatic process. TV drama is a highly technical representation of reality, not reality itself. An expert must work in a team, one which includes lights, cameras, actors and effects, to fit their own life experiences into the limits and conventions of the screen and create an effective illusion.

Thankfully, we were blessed with the generosity and talents of Philippa Lowthorpe as our director. Philippa immediately saw the value of close collaboration to create authentic births. Her key decision in Series One was to set aside dedicated rehearsal time for a birth scene before filming. It might surprise many that actors in TV drama don't usually rehearse. A cast in theatre enjoys weeks of rehearsal before opening night but TV actors generally turn up on the day and rehearse immediately before they shoot. Not here. *Call the Midwife* was going to spend the time to get Conchita's birth right.

We hired a room in the Bloomsbury Central Baptist Church in London. It had a few sparse props – a makeshift bed, a child's doll for a baby – but all the important elements were there. Terri, Philippa and the actors – Jess, Carolina and Tim. I sneaked a few bad photographs on my mobile phone and watched as they worked together to solve the problems they encountered – Philippa listening to Terri's advice, encouraging the actors, devising the right camera angles, the moments of dramatic focus, the essential sights and sounds.

Have you ever considered how difficult it is to film a birth without too much graphic detail? It's an event that takes place at what a midwife might euphemistically call the 'business end' of a woman's body – not exactly your normal Sunday-evening family location. TV has strict guidelines for what can be seen before 9 p.m. Blood must also be kept to a minimum, despite this being the most natural of human processes. But constraints can lead to real creativity. Philippa worked miracles in that room – devising how a baby might be filmed appearing using the angles, cutaways and reaction shots that would help a viewer fill in the gaps with their own imagination.

A key to viewers being transported by drama rests with the under-lying story and its skilful telling. Jess Raine had such a difficult journey to make as Jenny Lee in that first climactic birth. An inexperienced midwife, Jenny was assisting at a dangerous labour that would change her life; she was feeling every fear and emotion while needing to stay composed. Jess's reactions would guide us all as viewers through those key moments and what she achieved with her performance was a benchmark for all *Call the Midwife* performances to come. Those sights and sounds she witnessed in that room were felt by us all.

The sounds! Terri was a revelation. She knew better than anyone the extraordinary sounds a woman can make during labour – guttural, animal, primal and as far removed from Hollywood panting as you can imagine. Ageless but utterly human. Terri performed them for us and we listened, open-mouthed. How could we possibly present that to a Sunday audience? Yet Carolina took those sounds inside of her and made them Conchita's. Her performance was extraordinary.

In the final run-through, Carolina let rip with all she had. All the raw emotion, pain, love and passion. At the end of the scene there was a stunned silence. Nobody moved. I looked across the room and, to my surprise, I saw Terri, our real midwife, a hardened professional, who'd delivered literally hundreds of real infants in her long career, wiping tears from her face. She'd told me that birth usually made her cry. But this was just drama, make-believe. Why had she responded in that way now?

'Because it looked right,' she sniffed. 'It felt real.'

That was the moment I first suspected that *Call the Midwife* was a lot more than 'just' about babies being born.

HOW IT ALL BEGAN

Pippa Harris

Executive producer

Jennifer Worth had written three books about her time as a midwife in the East End of London in the 1950s. The first, *Call the Midwife*, was published as a small run of copies by a tiny specialist publishing house called Merton Books. Jennifer's agent thought it might have wider appeal and it was sent to us at Neal Street Productions as something that might make a good film. Our head of development at the time, Tara Cook, took it home to read and couldn't put it down. She passed it on to me and I found it fascinating – there was something that felt so immediate about the world described, but at the same time it was almost like reading Dickens or a historical novel. The level of poverty depicted was so extreme and so different to today, and yet it was only fifty years ago.

Jennifer had a real knack for episodic storytelling and was very good at vignettes, keeping you interested page by page. She was a natural observer, giving vivid descriptions of the people and medical situations she encountered in Poplar. You didn't always get a huge insight into her as a person, but you get a good sense of her as an intelligent, poised young woman looking at an unfamiliar world and trying to make sense of it. She was at the centre of an ensemble of fascinating characters and I thought that would make the book ideal for television.

FINDING THE WRITER

Pippa Harris

Executive producer

It can take a long time to find the right person to adapt a book for television. We often have to go to many different people and it can take months. In this instance, I had a gut instinct that Heidi Thomas would be perfect. We did our first jobs in television together, on *Soldier Soldier* – which was where we both met Annie Tricklebank as well, who has gone on to produce so many series of *Call the Midwife*. I knew that we needed someone who would understand the complexities of people's lives in Poplar and who would depict that world in an empathetic way. Heidi is extremely technically skilful and there was good raw material in the books but it wouldn't be like adapting a classic – there wasn't really a story. We needed someone who could structure that story and create a series that could run and run. I loved the way she'd adapted *Madame Bovary* and *Cranford* for television but I wasn't sure that she would be so keen on adapting the work of a living author. There's a freedom that comes with the author not being around!

Heidi Thomas

Writer and executive producer

When Pippa sent me Jennifer Worth's book I took one look at the cover and thought, 'That's not for me.' It had a photograph of some very scruffy urchins, which put it into a category that was known at the time as the 'misery memoir'. I'd just done *Cranford* and I was definitely thinking about nineteenth-century fiction rather than twentieth-century non-fiction. So it sat on my desk for six weeks until Pippa rang me up and said, 'Please, just read twenty pages.' I thought, 'Well, I can manage that.' So I did – and I got as far as page seventeen, where there was a description of a working-class East End woman giving birth and the narrator thought to herself: 'How much can she bear? How much can any woman bear?' In the middle of a very detailed description of a particular, physical event, something completely universal was expressed. At that point I didn't even bother carrying on – I just emailed Pippa and said, 'Yes.'

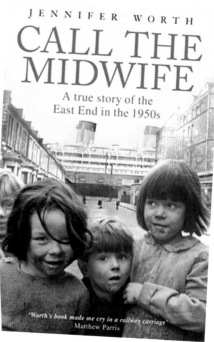

FROM PAGE TO SCREEN

Pippa Harris

Executive producer

Once Heidi was on board we had a project. We knew that medical stories work really well on television and that with the combination of nuns and nurses we had plenty of interesting characters. It was also important for Jennifer to be happy with our choice of writer, that she understood that Heidi would stick to the spirit of her books but that if it was a success we would need to run beyond those books, that we would run out of stories. Luckily, they got on very well.

Heidi Thomas

Writer and executive producer

I'd been looking for a new *Cranford* and, surprisingly, this was it. *Cranford* was a fictionalised memoir and the first volume of Jennifer's memoir was more fictionalised than is generally realised. She drew on other people's experiences as well as her own. What I quickly recognised was that what lay before me was something very rich with extraordinary potential, but it was complex – you could read three chapters and realise that it would make about ten minutes of television. Or you could read a paragraph that had such a complicated texture that it could make almost an entire episode.

My first meeting with Jennifer, along with her husband Philip, and with Pippa, was not a great success! We met at a rather swish fish restaurant in London where the acoustics were so bad that none of us could really hear what anyone was saying. Fortunately, it was followed up quite quickly by an invitation to lunch at their house in Hemel Hempstead. I remember it was a very snowy day and the roads were icy but they had a fire going in the living room,

dominated by an enormous Steinway grand piano that Jennifer played to concert standard. We talked and a friendship started to develop. When it came time to leave, she helped me on with my coat, which was navy blue with a very full skirt. Jennifer took a great interest in clothes and she buttoned me into that coat, remarking appreciatively on the lining – it felt like part of the audition process and that I'd passed.

Hugh Warren

Producer, Series 1–3

The producer's job is to act as a sort of creative marriage broker, making an environment and setting up a structure that enables other people to do the best work they possibly can. When a television show has been green-lit – given the go-ahead – in this case by the BBC, a producer is called in. My job then is to manage the production in all its details. There are lots of practical issues about how we can shoot and where we can shoot, proposing a designer and director, thinking about personal chemistry and who might work well with who, then basically making sure that they have the best resources available in terms of equipment, budget and location to flourish. It's a very collaborative process, particularly on a new show. So I was involved from the start in meetings with Heidi Thomas, Pippa Harris and the casting director, Andy Pryor. Overall, a producer's most important relationship is with the director and we were incredibly lucky to get Philippa Lowthorpe for the first series.

Another key person we got on board at the beginning was Eve Stewart as production designer. She made it possible for us to establish the whole feel and atmosphere of the East End of London in 1957, seen through the eyes of Jenny Lee, a young woman walking into a completely unfamiliar world. That opening sequence, as Jenny makes her way through the docks and into the heart of Poplar, seeing the poverty, the squalid conditions that people lived in, took up considerable resources in terms of the budget; it was hugely disproportionate but worth every penny. The programme immediately occupied somewhere real in people's imaginations. It had scale and life and after that you only needed to remind them – they knew the world that the characters inhabited.

We shot a lot in Chatham Dockyards, which was both fascinating and strange for me as my father and my brother had worked there. It served us very well as a location; we recreated whole streets, turning a 400-year-old dockyard into 1950s east London! The challenge always was to make sure it felt real, not a sanitised version.

CREATING THE WORLD

Eve Stewart

Production designer, Series 1–4

My background is theatre, which in many ways has stood me in very good stead for my work in television and film. I started off by thinking I wanted to do just fine art, but I so enjoyed every aspect of my foundation year at art school and was so lively and talkative that they ended up saying to me, 'You're too noisy for fine art! You can do a bit of everything, why don't you try theatre design?' So I did and that training led me to work with some brilliant directors – in particular Mike Leigh at the Hampstead Theatre and Peter Gill at the National Theatre Studio, doing workshops on new plays. Mike Leigh then asked me to work on his fabulous Gilbert and Sullivan film *Topsy Turvy*, and it all took off from there. As I didn't come into the business from film school, it's my background in theatre that informs the way I think. I try to make sure that every detail is right and the actors find that it really helps them to understand the world they're in.

I like to make sure that the right things are inside cupboards, even if the cupboards are never opened. And I've watched television programmes and noticed that the same lamps and cushions turn up every time – I was absolutely determined not to do that. I was born in the

26

East End, so I do know that world. And I also know women from an older generation who play spot the lamp! They'd let me know very quickly if I got anything wrong. A plastic bucket turned up in a shot once – I don't know how I missed that – and I was vilified. I got so many complaints it was if I'd killed someone!

We threw everything at that first shot of the docks and the Poplar streets. And I was so lucky to have Amy Roberts to work with as costume designer. Her family's from the East End as well so we both really understood that world. It meant that there was a backbone and a truth to what we did.

STEPPING INTO POPLAR

Heidi Thomas

Writer and executive producer

There was a wonderful period of working with Jennifer Worth. I'd go over to her house and we'd sit in what she called the Blue Room, not so much going through the book as having it there, as a shared property. She'd think back on her experiences and jot down notes in her spidery writing – you can still see that in the opening credits of the show. They weren't fully formed sentences, just bits and pieces she remembered, like 'Street games, skipping, children in go-karts made out of crates with old pram wheels attached' or 'Laundry hanging everywhere'. Those notes turned out to be the gift that kept on giving. I'd go back to them and find 'Cubs and scouts, youth clubs' – and they became essential elements of the society we ended up showing on screen. After she read my first draft, Jennifer only had one specific comment and that was about the cake that had to be hidden from Sister Monica Joan to prevent her from eating it all – it was hidden in a stewpot, not a cake tin!

Jennifer was a quick study and comprehended the process very rapidly. I'd never worked with a living writer before and I had huge respect for her and for her work. She knew that and it was a great moment when she said, 'I'm going to leave this to you now. You do what you think is right and I am sure it will be correct.' It was a two-way street and she was happy to have her brain picked. And she was very interested in how we were going to recreate the world of the East End that she remembered. She'd cycle up to 20 miles a day across the Isle of Dogs, over river bridges that are no longer there. Probably 80 per cent of the built environment she remembered no longer exists. We had to explain CGI – computer-generated imagery – to her and she was fascinated by that.

NONNATUS HOUSE

Hugh Warren

Producer, Series 1–3

Finding Nonnatus House was absolutely key to the first series. We were incredibly lucky to find a house in Mill Hill in north London – it was an old seminary with lots of different buildings that we could use. There's a great benefit when you're filming of being able to do a lot in one place. Because so many people are involved – in front of and behind the camera – it really helps if you're not moving the crew around all the time. There was a big chapel for the nuns, a kitchen and various other areas that worked really well. We knew that the site was owned by a developer but we thought it was worth the risk, that we'd have a bit longer there than turned out to be the case. After the second year, the owners wanted to start work on the development so we had to move on. That was a real challenge, losing that physical world after we'd worked so hard to establish it.

Heidi Thomas

Writer and executive producer

Before we started filming, during the pre-production process, Hugh Warren and Pippa Harris and I agreed to go with Jennifer Worth and her husband Philip to see the original Nonnatus House, where Jennifer had worked. It was called St Frideswide's Mission House, a big red-brick 1890s building on Lodore Street in Poplar. We agreed to meet at Aldgate tube station but the day before we got an email from Philip saying that Jennifer wasn't at all well. Within a week she had a diagnosis of terminal cancer. To this day I can remember reading that email and thinking, 'This was not in the scheme of things.' We were so looking forward to the pleasure she would derive from the filming and from the programme. She only lived another ten weeks; it was desperately sad. We needed, wanted her involvement but there was very little she was well enough to do.

JENNY AND JENNIFER

Heidi Thomas

Writer and executive producer

Jennifer loved the casting of Jessica Raine as Jenny Lee, her fictionalised self. They never met but we showed her pictures of Jessica and she definitely considered her to be appropriately beautiful and ladylike! Jennifer's books are a mixture of invention and reality – she didn't just write things down as journalistic facts; she was creative and imaginative and developed her characters, sometimes based on real people, sometimes not. Dr Turner was an invented character; Sister Monica Joan had elements of Monica Merlin, an actress who was Jennifer's lodger for a while. Sister Julienne was a real person, who remained friends with Jennifer for the rest of her life and wrote letters with little drawings in the margins to her two daughters.

In fact, Jennifer remained in touch with the whole of that religious community, to whom she gave the fictional name of the Order of St Raymond Nonnatus. She was a devout Anglican and used to stay with them and go on retreat. I have an uncle who's a priest and whose ministry was in Birmingham for a good fifteen years, so when I was doing my initial research I told him that I was trying to identify an order of Anglican nuns who had roots in community nursing and midwifery in the East End of London. He said, 'I know exactly who they are. They're the Order of St John the Divine and they're now based in Birmingham.' I asked Jennifer if that was correct and it was – with her permission we contacted them asking if we could visit for purposes of research and they were extraordinarily warm and welcoming.

Jessica Raine

Jenny Lee

I was so excited to start the journey. I'd begun my career in theatre and that grounding gave me confidence but I was unsure of how to work with the camera. It was the best experience to be in every scene, every day, leading a show and learning how to work with the camera. I loved it. I loved mapping Jenny's journey and being guided by Philippa Lowthorpe and working as a team.

I remember thinking that I had bombed the first audition. Someone told me (once I'd got the job!) that I nearly didn't get a re-call – thankfully Philippa saw something and the next audition was much better. I'll certainly never forget pretending to do a vaginal examination while sitting at a desk in the cold light of day. It was surreal and very funny.

I was already familiar with Jennifer Worth's original book, so felt I had a good grounding in the world it was portraying. Heidi's script really illuminated Jenny's naivety going into the poverty-stricken East End. We are introduced to that world and to the world of Nonnatus House through her eyes, so I knew it was a really special part that needed some grit and humour alongside the innocence.

Jenny needed to come over as young and inexperienced so I upped the RP (or poshness) of my accent and made my voice lighter than it is

G. LUMLEYS

2/6

TEA & COFFEE

230 HALLUM ST.

102 WOOLMORE ST.

IN ONE POUND

CANISTER

in real life. The uniform helped establish the character as well. It was so comfortable and I will forever be indebted to the costume designer, Amy Roberts, for that. And for Jenny's off-duty wardrobe, in which there were lots of lemony-yellow colours and cinched-in 'New Look' skirts and dresses that looked clean and prim. Jenny Lee always looked as if she left an aroma of fresh soap wherever she went.

Hugh Warren

Producer, Series 1–3

When I was asked by my agent if I would be interested in producing the show, I thought, 'Am I going to be able to engage with this, with these stories about midwives and babies in the 1950s? A gay man, with no children?' And then I recognised a universal theme that absolutely anyone can connect with – each story is ultimately about the triumph of love over adversity.

It's set in a period not long before I was born and within living memory for many people, but the world has changed almost beyond recognition since then. What was so important was to record that faithfully, not to pull away from the bleak, tough issues that Jennifer wrote about. She wrote about abuse, about illegal abortion, about terrible, grinding poverty. But however bleak, there was a redemptive quality. Having Jennifer's voice represented by Vanessa Redgrave as a sort of prologue and epilogue became a wonderful framing device that still represents that quality, all these years on.

HIT OR MISS

Philippa Lowthorpe

Director on Series 1–2

I was quite surprised to be asked to direct *Call the Midwife*. Much of my previous work had been in documentaries with pretty hard-hitting subjects and I'd directed *Five Daughters*, a drama series about the women who were murdered by a serial killer in Ipswich in 2006. Pippa Harris came beetling up to me at an awards event and said, 'I've got something for you.' I thought, 'Oh good, I wonder what it could be.' She sent me the books and I was immediately caught and held. It was the most amazing opportunity to put women giving birth on prime time television. Then I read Heidi's first script, almost without drawing breath, and I thought, 'This is going to be a hit.' She had written something that was rooted in the books and was authentic and real and at the same time a genuine drama. Heidi has this phenomenal ability to be funny one moment and heart-breaking the next, intimately moving and then powerfully angry. I couldn't believe my luck. I was asked to go and talk about it, a sort of interview, with Pippa, Heidi and Hugh Warren. It turned out to be the easiest interview I've ever done – I can't remember what I said, if anything, but Heidi talked nineteen to the dozen, Hugh smiled, Pippa smiled, and that was that.

Hugh put together the amazing design team of Eve Stewart on production and Amy Roberts on costumes. I was the lucky beneficiary of that and it was an extraordinary privilege to be there at the very beginning. Eve was someone I learnt a great deal from, about manipulating design and getting the right feel and atmosphere. Like Eve, Amy and I are both inveterate researchers and we all have extensive collections of photography books. There were phenomenal street photographers in the 1950s and 60s – Roger Mayne, who photographed children on a single street in west London over a period of five years, and Shirley Baker, who captured the lives of people in working-class, grindingly poor areas of Manchester. Their work proved inspirational.

Thanks to Heidi, Amy and I also went to Birmingham to visit the nuns of St John the Divine and got them to show us their wimples! We had lunch there and talking to them had a big influence on me – it made me really understand that part of the story: the nuns and the religious life, their devotion and the sincerity of their belief.

DELIVERY

Jessica Raine

Jenny Lee

The birth scenes were exhausting – not least for the actress performing the labour. I watched a lot of *One Born Every Minute* but I also think that growing up on a farm, watching animals giving birth and my dad helping deliver them prepared me for the pragmatic nature of portraying a midwife. There's no room for squeamishness, only the practical. The first scene we ever shot was the Conchita Warren storyline, about a woman who'd had twenty-four children. I was boiling 'urine' in a test tube, holding said test tube with a metal scissor contraption over a naked flame. It could not have been more 'proppy' and there was absolutely no room for nerves or shaky hands. It was the first labour and birth we filmed so we were all finding out what positions worked best for the most realistic portrayal. Later on, we discovered the use of knee pads – something I'm sure actual midwives would be grateful for! It was challenging and great fun. I particularly loved it when the real babies arrived – it massively focuses you when you are holding a perfect little baby.

SERIES TWO

1958

EPISODE ONE

Jenny's birthday trip to the cinema is soon forgotten as she's assigned to a complex case with expectant mum Molly Brignall, a victim of domestic abuse. Trixie and Sister Evangelina attend an unusual birth on a docked cargo ship, where the mother has been prostituted to the crew by her own father, the captain, and Dr Turner finds that his new gas and air machine is a big hit with Poplar's mums but an added burden for him.

EPISODE TWO

Cynthia is driven close to breakdown when the tragic death of a newborn baby she delivered leads to family suspicions and a legal investigation. Chummy signs up for missionary work in Africa but husband Peter needs Fred's help to get into shape – and Jenny's chance encounter with old flame Jimmy carries a sting in the tail when she discovers that his new partner is pregnant.

EPISODE THREE

Jenny is seconded to the London Hospital, and finds herself working under an abrasive male surgeon with a hidden vulnerability.

Meanwhile, the Nonnatuns face the unusual case of twin sisters Meg and Mave Carter who share a husband, but one of whom is now expecting. The eventful birth is a challenge to the twins' insular world as well as the whole team's medical skills. When Jimmy turns up at the London Hospital critically ill, Jenny faces a medical challenge of her own.

EPISODE FOUR

When Doug and Ruby Roberts's baby boy is born with spina bifida, his parents struggle to come to terms with their son's life-limiting condition and the child faces a future in an institution. The birth is a challenge for Jenny too, who has never delivered a child with such disability, or with such blighted prospects. Back at Nonnatus House, there is the hint of romance for the shy orderly Jane Sutton when eccentric Reverend Applebee-Thornton comes to stay.

EPISODE FIVE

The community prepares for the annual summer fête. Trixie secures a celebrity judge for the baby show but his intentions prove less than charitable towards her. Jenny struggles to reassure expectant mother Nora Harding, who is burdened by eight children already and dreading a ninth. Helpless and distraught, Nora takes illegal action to end her pregnancy, with disastrous consequences. Meanwhile, a surprise romantic encounter with Dr Turner leaves Sister Bernadette struggling with her feelings.

EPISODE SIX

With tuberculosis rife in the district, Dr Turner campaigns for one of the new mobile TB mass X-ray vans to visit Poplar, ably assisted by

Sister Bernadette. But their secret feelings are thrown into quiet turmoil when Sister Bernadette is discovered to carry the disease herself and is admitted to a sanitorium. Jenny, meanwhile, provides terminal TB care to a pugnacious old publican whose fractious relationship with his only surviving child, the heavily pregnant Julia Masterson, risks spurning a final chance for reconciliation.

EPISODE SEVEN

The return of Chummy and Peter to Poplar – along with the wonderful surprise that Chummy is pregnant. Jenny confronts the ugly side of the district when a Jamaican immigrant mum suffers racial abuse from her neighbours and Cynthia must deal with diabetic John Lacey, a deplorable domestic bully to his long-suffering wife Annie. Nonnatus House finds itself in possession of a new scooter, which Sister Evangelina and Fred take out for a hair-raising spin. At the sanitorium, a recovering Sister Bernadette comes to terms with her feelings for Dr Turner.

EPISODE EIGHT

Chummy and Peter prepare for imminent parenthood, while Fred has a visit from his daughter Dolly, who's also expecting. Sister Bernadette, now recovered, must decide where her future lies. Jimmy introduces Jenny to his friend Alec Jesmond and a trip out to a jazz club leads to a new romance. Nonnatus House is plunged into crisis when Chummy's labour develops serious problems, while Sister Bernadette's decision to check out of the sanitorium leads to an encounter with Dr Turner on a country road and a subsequent proposal. Chummy survives to welcome her own 'little bean' into the world and she and Dolly end the series with a double christening.

CHRISTMAS 1959

Festivities are thrown into chaos when an unexploded bomb is discovered close to Nonnatus House. The community's forced evacuation unites the entire team but exposes a young Korean War veteran's post-traumatic stress disorder and Trixie's own raw childhood experiences. Shelagh (Sister Bernadette) and Patrick's (Dr Turner) wedding plans are halted when Timothy falls dangerously ill with polio and a desperate bedside vigil ensues. When attempts to defuse the bomb fail, a premature explosion condemns the old Nonnatus House to demolition. Timothy pulls through and the team are able to celebrate the wedding of Patrick and Shelagh.

HAPPY RETURNS

Stephen McGann

Dr Turner

Spring 2012. Getting a second series had never been guaranteed, so when it happened it presented an interesting challenge for Heidi and the rest of us. The characters that had populated the first series would now have to expand to fit the greater space that our success had created. A more penetrating light would need to be shone on Nonnatus House and on the inner lives of all those who walked its corridors.

Laura Main and I discovered that the inner lives of Sister Bernadette and Dr Turner were about to undergo a particularly exciting and romantic expansion. We began Series Two as a religious sister and a widowed doctor with a young son but ended it with a car on a foggy road and a new love that led to wedding bells! It was a great privilege to play and an enormous pleasure to work on together.

Laura Main is a great friend, a fine colleague and model professional, whose brilliant attention to detail in Shelagh's complex journey from vocation to secular life was central to the success of Series Two. She also has a wicked laugh and tolerates my infantile humour with admirable generosity! So when I began to reflect on the journey Shelagh and Patrick made, who better to touch base with than my fellow traveller? Looking back, Laura and I laughed, reminisced and jogged each other's memories.

'What a gift that story was,' said Laura, 'and so unexpected! I'd been cast as a nun and here I was becoming somebody so different.'

Yet this transformation wasn't a foregone conclusion. We weren't told what was going to happen to us from one episode to the next. Only when the scripts arrived were we able to devour each new instalment! The fact that I'm married to the writer made no difference; Heidi never discloses plot details to me and so I find out my character's next steps when all the other actors do. But there was something rather beautiful about Shelagh and Patrick's storyline unfolding just like stories do in real life – over time. Slowly. Hesitatingly. With so much hiatus and uncertainty.

The uncertainty could be pretty stressful at times. 'We could never take anything for granted,' Laura remembered. 'We'd been told certain things but this was TV and details can always change. I remember on one particular day, our producer Hugh Warren came to my trailer full of nervous reassurance. I hadn't seen the latest script but he was worried that I had. "It's all right," he said, "you're not going to die." It was episode six, where Sister Bernadette is discovered to have TB. If Hugh hadn't said that, I would have been sure they were going to kill me off!'

As it happened, this was the twist that took Sister Bernadette away to the sanitorium and provided that final decisive moment in her journey – culminating in the romantic meeting on a wild, foggy road in episode eight. It was one of our great *Call the Midwife* moments. Funny thing was, it was never intended to be foggy at all! Director Minkie Spiro and her team had selected a rolling English landscape near Luton Hoo in Bedfordshire for full romantic effect. But when we all turned up that morning, you couldn't see further than twenty metres ahead! Yet that mist became the magical element that brought these two characters together – like their single future driving slowly into view through the haze of their previous lives. Filming can be a bit like that sometimes. You learn to make the best of what you have on the day, even if it's not what you thought you'd prefer. A bit like life, really . . .

One of the unforgettable elements in that scene, and in fact in all the key moments for Shelagh and Patrick in Series Two, was young

Timothy Turner, Dr Turner's son, played with brilliant cheek by a pre-teen Max Macmillan. Thinking back, both Laura and I were impressed by how the character of Timothy had become such a reference point for Sister Bernadette's growing love for Patrick. It was empathy for the motherless Timothy that had first emboldened her to share her own past with Patrick. It was Sister Bernadette who tended Timothy's injury when Patrick couldn't. It was Timothy and Sister Bernadette who took part in the three-legged race that ended with Patrick's fateful kiss in episode five. And it was Timothy who ultimately proposed to Shelagh, no longer Sister Bernadette, on his father's behalf – his letter wrapping the engagement ring – asking her, in effect, to be his mum. Timothy was the constant star helping Sister Bernadette navigate safely to her new life.

'It was two relationships,' said Laura, 'always. A mother's love, as well as a woman's love.' And a religious love, too. It should be remembered that Sister Bernadette leaves the Order but she never loses her love for God or her fellow sisters. Her love isn't something she withdraws from one place in order to reassign it elsewhere. It transforms into something more. Something re-confirmed and re-energised. And in that one character's journey you can detect a wider truth about *Call the Midwife* that I've always adored and, as a man, that I've always relished being a part of.

Call the Midwife has never been a drama simply about the ways in which women love men. Yes, there are those relationships in it but they've never defined its nature. *Call the Midwife* is, rather, a drama about the many interconnected ways that women can express love itself: for community, for God, for each other, for men, for their children, for themselves. These expressions of love can transform – can suffer upheaval, tragedy or pain – but always remain in the possession of the women who feel them.

Call the Midwife is a drama full of babies, but never just a 'baby drama'. It's a show about the women who have those babies. And the women who care for the women who have those babies. And all the many ways that love binds them, and defines them, and sets them free.

THE NUNS OF
NONNATUS

Jenny Agutter

Sister Julienne

What's fascinating about the series starting in 1957 is that the older nuns would have experienced two world wars. Sister Julienne might not have had such vivid memories of the First World War but Sister Monica Joan and Sister Evangelina certainly would. And that was brilliantly built into the storyline by Heidi, so that when we had to move from the first Nonnatus House, it was because of an unexploded bomb being found, leaving the foundations shaky. It was so clever to make those past dangers become present dangers. From the very start it meant that Sister Julienne was instrumental in finding a new building for the nuns and midwives and her office became the heartbeat of the place. Everything emanates from there.

Judy Parfitt

Sister Monica Joan

When I first joined the series I thought it was going to be for six weeks and that would probably be it. Having been brought up in a convent, I'd always wanted to play a nun and I loved the sound of Sister Monica Joan. Now it's gone on for so long and I say every year, 'Don't you want to get rid of me?' but we can't bear to finish her off. She is extraordinary – one minute she's quoting Keats and giving extremely sound advice, and the next minute she's wandering around in her nightdress going a bit doolally. My reasoning is that she comes from a good family and is extremely well educated but emotionally highly fragile. Anything that upsets her emotionally or physically can tip her into a dementia episode. She's very grand and considers it entirely normal that people will give her what she wants, including cake! I must say I rather miss the time when she went around nicking things off market stalls – that was enormous fun.

Pam Ferris

Sister Evangelina

Jennifer Worth's original book was the spark for me – when I read it, out of all the characters she described, Sister Evangelina was the one. Every time I talk about her, I feel moved by her. It wasn't hard to inhabit that amazing person – it was an honour. She'd grown up in a dirt-poor working-class family so she understood the people she worked with in the East End. I wanted to bring something to her that was deep and strong and tough.

There's a brilliant description by Jennifer Worth of an incident when Sister Evangelina was cycling back from the Isle of Dogs to Poplar and found that the road was closed because the swing bridges had been rotated to allow cargo boats to come through. She would either have had to wait at least half an hour or go back on her tracks and take a six-mile detour. She wasn't having that, so she hitched up her skirts, tucked them into her belt, yelled at a couple of dockers to give her a hand with her bike and jumped onto the nearest barge – there were eight or nine barges moored together and she made her way from one to the next to get to the other side. Wonderful.

Laura Main

Sister Bernadette

Being cast as a nun in the first series alongside three such incredible actresses was almost unbelievable for me. They were and are extraordinarily generous and I've learnt so much from them. We all look out for one another and I think it's something to do with the fact that we're portraying a group of people – nuns and midwives – who are kind and compassionate. I'm sure that influences us.

At the start, I had no clue that I would stop being a nun. There was just one moment, when the girls had all gone off to a dance and Sister Bernadette looks at herself in the mirror, removes her wimple, loosens her hair and finally takes her glasses off. The composer Peter Salem wrote a wonderful piece of music that became her theme. I remember thinking, 'Oh, there's more going on with her than I realised.' But it wasn't until the beginning of Series Two that I got a rough idea of what her future storyline was going to be and I thought, 'But I'm one of the nuns!' It was quite a shock.

THE FIRST FOUR

Jessica Raine

Jenny Lee

Bryony Hannah, Helen George and I were all pretty new to being on camera so it was fantastic to have each other for support. It always felt like a company to me – there was a constant mixing and matching of who you were acting with. And it really was a joy to be sitting at the table in Nonnatus House, listening to Pam Ferris and Judy Parfitt and Jenny Agutter chat about past jobs . . . illuminating! There are still moments now when I'm working on a scene and I remember something Pam said or did that helps me unlock it.

Helen George

Trixie Franklin

When I got the audition I read the book quite frantically – on the tube and on the bus, sobbing while I was reading, getting really into it. Then I went to the Neal Street Productions offices – quite intimidating with all their trophies on display – and did a scene a couple of times. I didn't think anything would come of it but then an offer came through a couple of weeks later. When I heard about who else was cast I could hardly believe it. It was so interesting at the beginning, not knowing how it would develop. Trixie and Cynthia were there to be Jenny Lee's aides in a way, to bring her out of herself. The medical side was touched on for Trixie in episode one but it wasn't until episode two or three that you saw her at work, not just having a cigarette in the kitchen or touching up her nail varnish. Trixie was there in the book, a part of the community, but fairly one-dimensional, so she's really Heidi's interpretation – she custom-made her for me!

Bryony Hannah

Cynthia Miller

Cynthia and Trixie were established at Nonnatus House when Jenny Lee arrived and the series started – they were already firm friends. They are incredibly different as characters but from the start you knew that they'd got each other's backs. I think that Cynthia was not long out of training and was still learning. All of us younger ones were dealing with childbirth on camera before we'd experienced it. It's strange and sad really that in our culture those experiences are still not freely shared. When the first series was aired, I was living in New Cross and I was stopped by a woman who had her son with her. He must have been ten or eleven and they watched it together. I remember thinking how wonderful that he would have some understanding, an insight into what it might be like for women to give birth.

When I auditioned for *Call the Midwife* I was in a play, *The Children's Hour*, doing matinees and evening shows, so I only had time to prepare for that – I read the book later on. The really unlikely thing was that the day I got the job, when I got the call to say I'd been offered the part, I was at Buckingham Palace! There was a big gathering for arts companies supported by the royal family.

Miranda Hart

Camilla Fortescue-Cholmeley-Browne/

Chummy

You never stop being a jobbing actor and being grateful when people see something in you, particularly when it's something beyond what they have seen you do before. Jennifer Worth wrote to me with a copy of the first book. She said in the letter that when she saw me on screen for the first time in *Miranda* she couldn't believe how much I reminded her of Chummy. I remember it was quite late when I opened the letter and I had an early call to film the next morning but I was so intrigued I went straight to the chapter in the book where Chummy makes an entrance. The way Jennifer describes her in the book is so funny and beautiful and I instantly thought, 'Right, no one else gets to play Chummy – I am in love!' I could of course see why she thought of me in terms of the physicality, but more importantly to me, I was immediately drawn to the story of this incredibly brave woman taking a stand against her upbringing and moving completely alone to follow her passion to a place she knew she wouldn't fit in and would have no understanding of. What a hero! I was lucky enough to be able to follow my childhood passion and I now have a passion for people following their passions! It's so important for people to be encouraged to be who they are but it takes a brave person to do it on their own, and Chummy did that. So for all sorts of reasons, before I had finished the book or read a script, I was all in.

LOVE IN THE MIST

Laura Main

Sister Bernadette

The two characters my character is closest to are played by the two actors I'm closest to: Sister Julienne/Jenny Agutter and Dr Turner/ Stephen McGann. As a nun, Sister Bernadette was in great need of advice and spiritual guidance and she always knew she could find that. It was so interesting that someone who was in a way hidden began to emerge into the light and discover that she might have a very different future.

There is such a supportive atmosphere on the show and nobody would ever be bumped off without warning or before they wanted to go. I don't think there would ever be that sort of ruthlessness just to make a sensation. When the storyline was that Sister Bernadette had got a shadow on her lungs and had to go to a sanitorium to be treated for TB, I was a little anxious, but as it turned out she recovered and then there she was, leaving the sanitorium, walking along a foggy road, lugging her suitcase, and Dr Turner's car appears out of the mist. Viewers were so behind that romance, it was really lovely. I feel I've had a major connection with young women, maybe in their late teens or early twenties. It was all over social media – we were #Turnadette!

Max Macmillan

Timothy Turner

That was one of my favourite moments, sitting in the car with Stephen – my dad, Dr Turner – driving around in the mist looking for Sister Bernadette sticking my head out of the window and screaming directions. The mist wasn't in the script – it was just luck on the day and it made it much more exciting!

MIDWIVES IN LITERATURE

Terri Coates

Midwifery advisor

I did my masters degree in 1997–98 and I was so keen to be reading novels rather than scientific papers that I suggested that maybe I could look at the way midwives are portrayed in fiction. They came out very badly – the two obvious examples being the untrained and generally drunk Mrs Gamp from *Martin Chuzzlewit* or the poor, long-suffering midwife in *Tristram Shandy*. It turned into an 8,000-word rant that I eventually boiled down to 1,500 words for an article in the *Royal College of Midwives Journal* in January 1998 in which I said that somebody needed to do for midwives what James Herriot had done for vets with *All Creatures Great and Small*. There is everything in midwifery – love and birth and sex and death – ready and waiting for a really good block-buster.

Jennifer Worth read the article and said that it inspired her to write her memoirs. She contacted me and sent a few handwritten chapters. She'd only been a midwife for a short time and had forgotten a lot and I asked her if she'd like me to correct the midwifery details and in due course an entire manuscript arrived. At the time, I was a Midwifery Course Director at Southbank University, with a department to run and post-graduate student's assignments to correct, but her stories leapt off the page and I ended up working with her over a period of fifteen years. I started training as a midwife in the early 1970s so I was taught by people who were probably in clinical practice when *Call the Midwife* was set. It was easy for me to go back to them and say, 'Look, we do this now – how did you do it then?' And I found textbooks from the appropriate period to use for reference.

SERIES THREE

1959

EPISODE ONE

As Series Three opens, the team move into the new Nonnatus House and we meet Sister Winifred. Chummy is finding it difficult to adjust to married life without midwifery, while the team are finding it hard to raise awareness for their new weekly clinic. There's a medical mystery as Dr Turner can't work out what's wrong with Merle Vickers's two sickly children, although Sister Monica Joan is adamant that the answer lies in her old medical book. Chummy helps the clinic by arranging an official visit by Princess Margaret, while Sister Monica Joan's insight leads to a diagnosis of cystic fibrosis in the Vickers family.

EPISODE TWO

Jenny's promotion to nursing sister over the more experienced Trixie leads to resentment. Cynthia wants to adopt new relaxation techniques for mothers during childbirth but Sister Evangelina is sceptical. Jenny cares for expectant mum Doris Aston, who reveals that the child she is carrying – the result of an affair – must be kept from her aggressive husband. She contemplates abandoning the infant but Jenny helps her to pursue formal adoption after the truth is exposed. Cynthia's success at calming a distressed mother in labour earns Sister Evangelina's belated praise.

EPISODE THREE

Sister Julienne and Trixie take a trip behind bars to care for pregnant prison inmate Stella Crangle, who wants a better life for her child but fears it will be taken away from her. Shelagh and Patrick's plans for a family are devastated by news that Shelagh's past TB has rendered her unable to conceive. Fred secures theatre tickets as a treat for Chummy's birthday but plans change when they turn out to be counterfeit. Sister Julienne takes up Stella's case with the prison board and eventually finds the work and accommodation that means she'll be able to keep her baby on release.

EPISODE FOUR

Jenny's boyfriend Alec invites her to spend a weekend away in Brighton but Jenny, doubtful of his intentions, cancels. Shelagh, devastated by her infertility news, throws her energies into reforming a choral society. Sister Winifred helps Leah Moss's mother, Tzirale, a Holocaust survivor, escape the flat she's been confined to for twelve years. Disaster strikes when Alec is involved in a terrible warehouse accident and unexpectedly dies due to complications from his injury. Shelagh's choir provides the music for a moving funeral and a grief-stricken Jenny departs on compassionate leave.

EPISODE FIVE

When Sister Julienne falls ill, Shelagh takes over the running of Nonnatus House and we welcome Patsy Mount onto the midwife team. Sister Evangelina is refusing to celebrate the anniversary of her vows but preparations reveal a private family pain. There's scandal at a residential home when Sally Harper, a woman with Down's syndrome, becomes pregnant. The family suspect a staff member but Sally has formed a tender relationship with Jacob Milligan, another resident at the home. After Sally's baby is stillborn, and despite the couple's protests, Jacob is moved to a home in Scotland. Timothy Turner finally gets his polio calipers removed in time for Sister Evangelina's Jubilee celebrations.

EPISODE SIX

Patsy's brusque manner gets her into trouble at the clinic and she is removed from midwifery duties and placed on district rounds. Meanwhile, Trixie is delighted when handsome curate Tom Hereward invites her to a cricket match but the outing turns out to be less romantic than she had hoped, with a troop of Cubs on a broken-down bus. A positive encounter with the mother of an adopted child inspires Shelagh to investigate adoption for her and Patrick. Trixie helps two Northern Irish runaways from opposite sides of the sectarian divide, while Patsy successfully diagnoses a tropical disease contracted by an old soldier in a prisoner-of-war camp, due to her own childhood experiences of internment by the Japanese.

EPISODE SEVEN

Jenny returns to work at the London Hospital where the impersonal approach to midwifery challenges her compassionate instincts. Chummy's disdainful mother arrives as a reluctant guest at the Noakes's home, while Sister Julienne and Cynthia care for a young mother, Pamela Saint, who develops post-natal psychosis, with almost disastrous consequences for mother and child. Shelagh's adoption plans are jeopardised when background checks reveal Dr Turner's own past problems with mental health. Pamela is admitted for electroconvulsive treatment. Chummy is shocked to discover that the cancer her mother has been hiding is untreatable.

EPISODE EIGHT

Chummy nurses her dying mother at home, helped by her colleagues and friends. Shelagh and Patrick are delighted to be approved for adoption. Shelagh's choir enters a competition, while Jenny is tested to her limit in a particularly long and arduous birth, followed by a visit to Chummy's mother's bedside – a visit that crystallises her need for a new start in hospice care. A sudden agency call sees Shelagh and Patrick united with their new adopted daughter. The choir is triumphant, Trixie and Tom kiss and Jenny leaves Nonnatus House for the final time.

CHRISTMAS 1959

When harsh practices are exposed at a local home for unmarried expectant mothers, Chummy and Patsy come to the rescue of the inmates and help a single young mum to keep her child. Cynthia is involved in the distressing case of impoverished former mental-asylum inmates Nancy and Victor, who believe they are expecting a child. It's revealed that Nancy was sterilised and lobotomised without consent by the asylum surgeons – yet their enduring love spurs Cynthia to pursue a new life as a nun and she leaves Nonnatus House to become a postulant.

A NEW HOME

Stephen McGann

Dr Turner

The third series of *Call the Midwife* was an important milestone for us. Series Two had been another big hit and we were now clearly part of the British television landscape. But the milestone we faced concerned our physical landscape too and not just the media one. Towards the end of filming the second series, we heard rumours that our prime Nonnatus House location at the disued St Joseph's Seminary in London's Mill Hill was to be sold and developed for luxury housing. This meant that we were effectively homeless.

Fortunately, Heidi had anticipated the approaching problem and had woven an ingenious plot into the preceding series' Christmas special. An unexploded wartime bomb had threatened the Poplar neighbourhood with its eventual explosion, rendering Nonnatus House structurally unsound. The convent had to find a new home.

Well, that was the story sorted. But where were we going to find a location building as evocative as St Joseph's? To be honest, the old place had been pretty grim to work in. It looked marvellous on screen but it had no internal power, rampant rot, inches of dust and collapsing ceilings. Our unit base outside was in a sloping, muddy field that turned into a slippery quagmire as soon as it rained. Television drama is an industry of make-believe, an alchemist's trick of lighting and art design that turns derelict buildings into gold. The reality behind the camera is usually chemical toilets, freezing night shoots and dripping rafters. If the end result of period drama is an elegant swan, then the cast and crew making it are the soggy webbed feet paddling away in the weeds . . .

Not that our new location needed to be a luxury hotel. The important thing was that it should evoke the same faded elegance and religious austerity that characterised the community we represented. The news finally came through from our producer, Hugh Warren, that an ideal new Nonnatus House had been found – part of the Longcross film studio complex in Chertsey, Surrey. It was called Barrow Hills, an Edwardian country house and wartime officers' mess – a rambling, spooky warren of servants' rooms, stucco ceilings, long corridors and lavish oak panelling. Cold. Dark. Dusty. And our much-loved home ever since.

A key advantage to moving into a proper film studio like Longcross was that we could build more of our own secure locations – outside, as well as indoors. When the cast first arrived, we were thrilled to see the magic that the art department had worked on the place. Not only was the house entrance decked out with a rather grand convent porch but in front of it we had our own Poplar street with terraced housing, allotments, shops – even a railway underpass! It felt permanent and secure, and that we had a proper future.

Barrow Hills house, like St Joseph's before it, is a faded and bare-bones kind of place. With no domestic power of its own, it can be rather forbidding once the crew turn the generators off at the end of a day. And it has such a labyrinth of corridors and rooms that I still manage to get lost in the old place after all these years! But back in 2013, those many rooms were pure gold. They could be transformed to provide us with countless different domestic and clinical settings. Most impressive at Barrow Hills were our new permanent sets – the iconic backdrops that define *Call the Midwife* to this day: the Nonnatus House dining room and entrance corridor, Sister Julienne's office, the nurses' clinical room, even Dr Turner's maternity home and surgery. The actors, when

not needed on set, were now able spend their time in warm location caravans a short walk away, close to the make-up and costume trailers, parked on clean tarmac. No more wading through Mill Hill mud baths to get to the catering bus!

When we needed larger locations to film in, such as Series Three's new community clinic, we could use the main studios on the other side of Longcross to build what we needed, rather than depend on outside locations and their private owners. Longcross studios has an interesting history: it was originally a military engineering base for the development of tanks. So there was a wealth of functional post-war building stock that could double as 1950s municipal Poplar.

Not that we didn't still venture out to film beyond the studio. Those quintessential cycling street scenes beneath the hung washing lines in *Call the Midwife* were still filmed at Chatham's Historic Dockyard in Kent. When poor Alec fell from the staircase in episode four and when Pamela Saint, her mind ravaged by psychosis, prepared to throw herself and her child into the Thames in episode seven, all the action was filmed next to the River Medway at Kent's historic docks. This vast public museum has an unrivalled collection of dockland buildings that perfectly evoke the post-war world of Poplar. The real East End has few of those old buildings left, having been substantially redeveloped over the decades.

Yet there is always something special about those times when we *are* able to go back into the real East End to film. It has always felt like coming home, despite our main filming home now being established far away in leafy Surrey. Those streets outside of Chummy and Peter's house? They're in the East End. And when we require a church to mark those great moments in the lives of our characters – the births, marriages and deaths – we return to the wonderful St Anne's church in Limehouse, just a short distance from where the real Poplar midwives did their work.

Our new home in 2013 meant many things to us. It was the feeling of security – the idea that we had a future in a drama landscape where nothing ever felt completely certain. It was the thrill that every new homeowner feels – the ability to put our own stamp on a new building and watch it transform to fit all of our dreams and ambitions. Most of all, it was the essential foundation for all the things that were to come. A new shore, where those paddling swan's feet could find some solid ground to walk on.

KEEPING IT REAL

Beverley Gerard

Standby art director, Series 1–3

I was brought onto the show by Eve Stewart, the production designer, who I'd worked with on *Upstairs, Downstairs*. The standby art director is the only member of the art department who is present during filming, on set for every single scene, every take. You have to work with the director of photography – DP – and camera operator to make sure that each shot is the best it can be, and it's your responsibility to maintain the sets, keeping everything looking exactly as it should. There's a big cross-over with the props department. We'd dress the sets together on days of filming, going in with the props early in the morning and making sure everything was there. It needs to be very collaborative. On *Call the Midwife*, I was given free rein, which isn't always the case; I was allowed to really read and interpret the characters for myself, which is something I love to do. That means gathering together the items that a person would have, their possessions – powder compact, magazines and books, family photographs they might put by their bed. We built a huge collection of props, a great stockpile of things from the 1950s on. I was always on the lookout for things, spotting bits and pieces at vintage fairs.

When the nurses in a particular scene were packing their bags to go out on a job I'd sometimes have to get someone to watch one person while I watched another. If they had to do the scene again you'd have to say, 'Stop! Last time you picked that up in your right hand and then that in your left.' We made things as easy as we possibly could but they had to learn how to hold the medical instruments and look completely comfortable with them. They couldn't pick something up and look as if they didn't know which end to hold.

Getting the detail right pays off, though. I've got a friend who's a nurse and she'd never watched it till lockdown, when she binged on the whole thing from episode one. She couldn't get over how accurate the detail was and how professional they all looked. One of the most difficult things we had to do was show a baby that was born in a caul, still inside an intact amniotic sac. It was a prosthetic baby and every time we went to place it on the bed the sac would burst and I had to say, 'Sorry, we'll have to start again.' And the actress had to get out of the bed, and we'd change the sheets and start all over.

MILL HILL TO LONGCROSS

Jenny Agutter

Sister Julienne

The move from Mill Hill to Longcross was quite an upheaval but we had such a strong team of people throughout. Certainly we couldn't have done it without Hugh Warren's support, finding the new location and getting us there. Then Annie Tricklebank, who took over as producer, carrying on from him. She's one of those people who's absolutely calm and gentle and makes decisions. Then that's it, everything suddenly becomes much easier. I'm such a prevaricator – always looking at different options. Maybe we could do this, maybe that! Her certainty and care have carried us through.

Sister Julienne's office in the new Nonnatus House became something at the very core of the community. It's a place where people can bring their problems, discuss any issues that may arise. I have to say, I've become very attached to it myself. When Sister Julienne came back from South Africa in Series Six to find she'd been replaced by this rather beady matriarch of a Sister, played by Harriet Walter, it shook me a bit as an actress. It was terrible not having my central place. Fortunately, I've got it back again now.

Pam Ferris

Sister Evangelina

The first location for Nonnatus House was the most extraordinary place. It was falling to bits; it rained inside some of the rooms and sometimes worse – pigeon poo suddenly splatting down. It was hard to film there and really unpleasant at times but the atmosphere was perfect, exactly right. We squeezed in and got on with it and that was helped by the fact that we were such a good team – and mostly women. Having a female director was still, only ten years ago, a new and rare experience. From a professional point of view, it was a lot quieter. If we were ten people sitting around a table and shooting a scene, you could actually hear yourself think. We'd chat quietly when we were free and there was a terrific focus, really lovely.

Eve Stewart

Production designer, Series 1–4

We didn't need to build that much for the first series – we were really lucky to get St Joseph's in Mill Hill and be able to take it over and create different rooms within the space. Then we urgently had to find somewhere else and, after an extensive search, found this old house by a racetrack in Longcross. It was a house on its own, which was just what we needed, but it needed a street opposite and we had to create that. I did a lot of investigating – the people on *EastEnders* let me have a good look around to see what was working for them and what wasn't. A lot of that set's made of plaster, which needs endless fixing and repairing. A construction manager I knew suggested that we make the frontages of the street out of resin, which is really tough and would hold its structure. So we found a little house in Poplar, next to the original Nonnatus House where Jennifer Worth worked, and got permission to take a squeeze. That means painting the whole thing with rubbery stuff and taking a cast of the entire house. That could then be reproduced and we ended up with these 30-foot-tall structures, into which we could put doors and windows. They've lasted really well – they're still using them.

BIKING ABOUT

Jessica Raine

Jenny Lee

It was so much cycling! When we were in Chatham doing all the exterior scenes those cobbles had pretty deep grooves between them so if your front wheel got caught in one of them it was a nightmare. You just had to battle through. When I was cycling along I was always thinking, 'Is my face juddering and wobbling about, like it does when people go at high speed?' Everyone would assure me – 'No, no, it's fine, it looks great.' Basically that was all I was thinking – that and not toppling off!

Pam Ferris

Sister Evangelina

Those bikes were really heavy and my shoes were so big on me that they didn't allow me to turn the bike because my foot would hit the front wheel. Add in darkness and cobbles and puddles with holes underneath that you didn't know about and it was a risk to life and limb – in my case to my cruciate ligament. I ended up having to have an operation on my knee. But I loved it when I was going straight.

Miranda Hart

Chummy

I found acting not being able to ride a bicycle *very* hard because I am really good at cycling! The year before joining *Call the Midwife*, I had done a Comic Relief John o' Groats to Land's End challenge so had trained to ride a racing bike. To be not good at something you are good at is strangely odd, though I suppose because my balance was good I could wobble well. And riding her bicycle into PC Noakes and knocking him over was, I suppose, how Chummy got her man!

POPLAR STREETS

Ben Caplan

PC Peter Noakes

PC Noakes was a link between Nonnatus House and the Poplar streets. He was an absolute joy to play and I remember how excited I was when I read the first few episodes. Heidi's writing comes off the page so easily and when you've got a really good script like that it makes your job much easier. You need to trust it, to play it tenderly and carefully and simply, and then everything just falls into place. When I met Miranda and we had a read-through, there was an immediate chemistry – we didn't have to do loads of work to manufacture that.

Eve Stewart

Production designer, Series 1–4

It was extremely important to create a world that looked and felt real. There was terrible poverty in the East End in the 1950s and we had to

show that. Windows couldn't look too clean, taps had to drip, washing had to be hung up indoors as well as in the street where in winter nappies would freeze on the line. People had outside loos or shared one on a tenement staircase.

With the interiors we did have to try very hard not to make everything brown. Wallpaper patterns and paint colours hadn't changed much since the 1920s. After the Second World War, because of a shortage of pigment, a lot of paint companies would throw everything into a big vat just to get enough paint. That's why you got so much of that sludgy brown. When we were painting the sets, someone would say, 'OK, what colour are we using?' and we'd all laugh. 'Shit brown again?'

BABY HANDLING

Terri Coates

Midwifery advisor

Some portrayals of labour and birth on television give a very false idea of what actually happens. If you were growing up in a tenement in the 1950s you would have been aware of pregnancy and birth and new babies. Now these things happen behind closed doors and it can come as something of a shock.

On *Call the Midwife* we work really hard to make it look as realistic as possible and for that reason we do need very small babies, only a few days old. At the beginning we asked around local maternity units but now there are agencies who provide them and a lot of parents are keen for their babies to be on the show. Until quite recently I was in clinical practice in Salisbury and I've had nearly forty years in practice altogether so I'm pretty relaxed around mothers and newborns. I remain calm instinctively when I'm holding a baby – then the baby stays calm as well. A lot of it is preparing parents for what they should expect. They often think that the filming process will be very glamorous and it's anything but. The money is put in front of the camera so behind it everything can seem a bit scruffy. I make sure that everything is clean and warm and safe, and I take people to see the set before we bring the baby in. I'm used to working with anxious new parents. It's all done very gently.

Pam Ferris

Sister Evangelina

Terri was such a help – she was a great presence on set and I learnt an awful lot about the whole process from her. She gave us all the confidence we needed when we were handling the babies. It's so true that a baby can tell if you're uncertain or tentative – it tenses up and the next thing you know it'll start to cry. They loved it when they felt safe and comfortable and I enjoyed it tremendously. It was one of the best bonuses of the job.

Miranda Hart

Chummy

Now I won't lie, I am not a massive baby person, but seeing the babies through Chummy's eyes really gave me a perspective on the miracle of life and birth and I began to see a newborn child in a new way. Delivering a baby, however (it may shock people to hear), I had never done that . . . So yes, it was a relief that Chummy was nervous handling a breech birth on her own! I remember the room would spin after they called cut because I was hyperventilating acting Chummy's nerves and then kind of holding my breath as myself, acting with a tiny baby covered in oil that I REALLY did not want to drop! So I was a mess after that scene.

I don't think I learnt many skills that would help if someone went into labour in my presence – mainly because I can only work with equipment from the 1950s! Although if you ask my family, I am excellent in an emergency. I come into my own, strangely. Basically, I am good in a very serious situation or in a very playful, clowny one – I don't bother with the in-between boring normalness of life.

Bryony Hannah

Cynthia Miller

———————

I wasn't familiar with tiny babies – I might have changed one nappy – and I felt a great responsibility. On Series One we all had to wear these rubber gloves and there were no small ones. It was so hard – I was trying to cut the cord in these ginormous gloves and kept on dropping the scissors. One of the first births we filmed, we did the whole birth without the baby before the baby was brought onto the set. I had it in my arms and was jogging it up and down and Terri Coates said, 'Calm down, calm down – you weren't doing that before!' She taught us to hold the baby very firmly, close to us, so that it felt secure and could hear your heartbeat.

STARTLINGLY COMPETENT

Emerald Fennell

Patsy Mount

My first appearance was as a guest and I auditioned for one appearance in one episode, which was just as well because it wasn't quite as frightening as auditioning to be a regular member of the cast – if I'd been doing that I'd almost certainly have been too nervous and completely blown it. It was wonderful to be asked to join, even though it was nerve-wracking coming into a show where everyone already knew each other and had an intimate working relationship. But Bryony and Helen, in particular, were determined to make me feel welcome and supported, and from the get-go it was very clear that the cast members would all rely on each other and trust one another.

It was fun to perform a character who was super competent. I'm really incompetent and anxious myself, and would be the most terrible nurse in the world! Patsy was so straightforward and tactless. She had plenty of lovable characteristics, but she stepped on everyone's toes when she first arrived. Heidi sent me an A4 page describing Patsy and who she was, so I knew she was gay and I knew that her brusqueness and apparent lack of emotion was due to having survived something very difficult. I didn't know what that was specifically. The day when she revealed that she and her family had been in a Japanese prisoner-of-war camp was quite something. I had to learn the speech on the fly because the schedule got swapped around at the last minute. It's the kind of thing that you want time for, to let it become ingrained, but in a funny way it was better not to have spent too much time analysing.

None of us younger ones had children at that time, but quite a few of us have given birth since. It's an interesting dynamic – I would say I ended up knowing almost too much! Because *Call the Midwife* is a drama it often focuses on things that can go wrong, but it's not a bad thing to be equipped with that information. It's a dangerous, tough thing that women do, and that's very powerful. It's extraordinary to me that you still come across men who will say something like, 'Oh my wife loves the show but I can't watch it,' and I'd sometimes say, 'Why? Presumably you watch people getting murdered on screen, or people at war getting their legs blown off – what is it about women doing something brave and bloody that freaks you out?' It interests me that there can still be that response. Women's lives are obviously as rich and dark and frightening as men's are and we still don't see enough of that. *Call the Midwife* has proved over and over again how important it is to show that and has an astonishing, far-reaching popularity. Luckily for me I had an agent who only ever wanted me to go for things that were difficult and interesting, so I ended up playing a competent, complicated nurse-midwife rather than 'Girlfriend no. 4' or 'topless mermaid'.

I've never before or since been on a show for such a long period of time – it's as close as an actor gets to a day job. Because of having this very fixed schedule, knowing that for six months you'd be working and then you'd have a six-month gap, you could use the time wisely. Every year in the hiatus, after finishing a series of *Call the Midwife*, I'd write a book – so those two things are completely intertwined for me. But the really wonderful thing was that I was able to learn so much. If you're interested in how the filming process works, you couldn't be in a better place to watch. I'd been wanting to direct for a long time, but I needed to work out how to do it. My first short film, that really set everything going for me, was *Careful How You Go*, and it was full of people from

Call the Midwife – including the fabulous Linda Bassett and Charlotte Ritchie. When I was playing Patsy I had four years of watching people work – different directors with different methods and approaches, but with a consistency of both cast and crew, all of them incredibly busy but also incredibly generous with their time. People like Paddy Blake, the camera operator, who would always tell me what lens he was using. That kind of schooling was invaluable.

MAKE DO
AND MEND

Amy Roberts

Costume designer, Series 1–2

It was wonderful to start in 1957 and to research that period in detail. People are bigger now and a different shape, mostly because of better nutrition and different types of exercise, so although some of the actresses are very slender we couldn't always use vintage clothes. What was important to me was to serve that community – my mum's from the East End and my grandfather was a dockworker in Custom House so it was up to me to do the family proud and get it right. Very few clothes would have been new. There just wasn't the money so people would have one pair of shoes that had to be repaired, soled and heeled over and over again. If a collar was worn out you'd unpick it and turn it around. If a jumper got holes in, you'd unravel it and use the wool to make a new one. We were able to source quite a lot of original fabric but if it hadn't been used we'd wash it to death and dip it, dye it, break it down, soften it, patch it. And with shoes we'd age them and soften them, make them look properly worn in.

Undergarments need to be right too, even if you never see them. Pointy bras in early episodes and pantie girdles with suspender belts for stockings, which were usually darned or had ladders in them. And the

poorest people had to go bare-legged even in winter. Small children would just have jumpers on and nothing else and would relieve themselves in the gutter, which we couldn't really do in a primetime BBC series! The nuns had to have proper sensible underwear, big bras and knickers, and black stockings – I made them wear proper stockings for authenticity but may have relented on Series Two and cheated with tights.

Jennifer Worth loved clothes and was very elegant, slim and trim, so she was an inspiration for Jenny Lee's clothes. It was fun with the girls to be able to think about their personalities and what they would have worn when they weren't in uniform. Trixie of course became an aspirational fashion figure but it had to be plausible, given the sort of salary she would have been earning as a young midwife. We showed her working out how to look good on a limited income – her ideas would have come from magazines and films. The film stars of that day were photographed socially, at parties and nightclubs, so they were role models for style.

Jenny Lee was from a different, middle-class background and for her first appearance, walking through the docks to Nonnatus House, we wanted her to stand out, to be pale and clean and beautiful, surrounded by workers who were dirty and sweaty, in dark greys and blues. She was a creature from another world, a neat, controlled, inexperienced girl thrown in at the deep end. As the series progressed, you saw what a journey she had embarked on – she learns a lot about life and humanity, and gets rid of her prejudices along the way.

For the nurses' uniforms I had a photograph of Jennifer that gave me a kickstart, but it was in black and white. Colour-wise, I wanted something that contrasted well with the dark browns and greens of the interiors at Nonnatus House and my choice of colours was a nod to the blue and maroon of West Ham, the East End football team. I really enjoyed doing that! Then they had little white Peter Pan collars that they would have taken off to wash. You could see them hanging on an airing horse in their bedrooms along with pairs of stockings.

The nuns' habits were closely modelled on what the nuns of St John the Divine in Birmingham wore. They were so kind and showed us absolutely everything. In fact, they even gave me a wimple and veil with that little chin strap. The veils were short for practical reasons, so they didn't get in the way. It was quite tricky getting them to fit comfortably and look all right on camera. Judy Parfitt was absolutely wonderful and so funny. She said, 'I know I've got to be a nun and I'm going to look horrible, so just do it,' and she'd never look at herself in the mirror. At the end of Series One, when we'd shot her last scene, she came off set and started stripping as she walked up the hill to her trailer. She took off the headpiece, the chin strap, the little cap, her top layer. Everyone was in fits – the lighting guys, crew, everyone. She got to the trailer, pulled open the door as she got to the base layer, revealed one very long and elegant leg for a brief moment – and slammed the door behind her! Such style.

HEADGEAR

Pam Ferris

Sister Evangelina

You do sacrifice your vanity when you put on a wimple, but it was one of the reasons I wanted to do the role. I've lost count of the lunchbreaks I've lost or had shortened to almost nothing because of having to be in make-up, having my hair done or getting my wig tweaked. Without all that, you're straight in and out and the acting becomes the important thing. I think it was in Series Two that someone thought the wimples looked too floppy – at least the veil bit at the back. So they were starched to look better but, as a result, the wimples created a funnel of sound and flattened our ears so we lost the echo chamber and found it impossible to hear properly.

Also, I wanted my costume to look lived in, not ironed and beautifully presented every day. The costume people were so efficient and hard-working but I had to ask them to stop, let my habit get a bit frayed and faded from being washed so often.

Amy Roberts

Costume designer, Series 1–2

Getting the nurses' headgear right was important – little white, folded caps when working at the mother and baby clinic and the dark red felt hats they wore outside, on the backs of their heads. We sewed little hooks inside the hatband so you could put kirby grips through and into the hair to keep them in place. Chummy's mother was frightfully grand and we gave her some marvellous great hats made out of birds' feathers and netting.

MOTHER TROUBLE

Miranda Hart

Chummy

I wanted Chummy's story to be one that people could identify with despite her upbringing and the different era. My concern was that everyone would expect a jolly-hockeysticks type but I instinctively knew I didn't want to play her like that. I wanted her to be more softly spoken than her physical appearance and clumsiness might indicate, breaking up her sentences a little bit, almost like she was nervous to finish them or surprised that someone would want her to keep going. That was my access point to feel her vulnerability, and it was her vulnerability I wanted to play. Feeling a fish out of water is something everyone has experienced to one degree or another and we all want to find the confidence to be ourselves, to have a romantic and fulfilling relationship and find meaning and purpose in life. And my beloved Chummy, God bless her – and let's not forget this was a REAL WOMAN – achieved all that. She grew into professional and personal confidence and the world was a better place for it. That's the most important part of her story to me, to show that when we dare to be who we are made to be, it not only makes our own lives fuller but brings change around us.

Her relationship with her mother challenged all that and the episode when she died, sublimely written by Heidi, was extraordinary and very moving to perform. I will never forget that day on set, actually – it was when I understood where the phrase 'Don't look me in the eyes' comes from. It's a phrase that's often bandied about as a joke in terms of being such a diva that you won't allow people to look you in the eye. But that day I realised it was about needing to concentrate. I so wanted to do that scene well, and you had to get yourself into a particular place emotionally to do it justice. We were filming in this TINY room, everyone on top of each other, chatting away, and before it was time to turn the cameras around on me I just had to look at the floor and not make eye contact with anyone as I didn't want to break the spell of where I had been in the scene.

But that scene for me wasn't as much about her mother dying as about Chummy being, for the first time, connected to and loved by her, the one person she wanted to be loved by all her life. That was what was so moving. I'm welling up now, just thinking about it – but that's what Chummy does to me. She's so brave and noble and honourable that the memory of playing her can never not be moving to me. That, mixed up with all the laughs on set with the most wonderful cast – those are memories that I will, genuinely, treasure for ever. I cannot believe how lucky I was to have been part of it. Right, I'm off to find a tissue . . .

SERIES FOUR

1 9 6 0

EPISODE ONE

The series opens with the arrival of new nurse Barbara Gilbert. She makes a bad start, after a boozy welcome party with Trixie and Patsy leaves her with an aching head and facing Sister Evangelina's hardest stare. Yet her deft handling of a nervous mother with a premature baby earns the old nun's respect. Trixie deals with an appalling case of child neglect – a young boy, Gary Teeman, is discovered caring for his little siblings in unspeakable squalor. With Trixie's care the Teemans are rescued, de-loused and placed for adoption. Tom is deeply moved by her actions and proposes. Trixie accepts – but the case has opened old wounds.

EPISODE TWO

The indomitable Phyllis Crane joins Nonnatus – but her officious manner puts the team on edge. A rich benefactor wants to support the convent, but Sister Julienne is conflicted when it's revealed to be a man with whom she had a romantic relationship before her vocation. There's anguish when Barbara and Patsy deliver a stillborn child to a young Trinidadian mother, but a healthy twin is saved and Phyllis's softer side shows through. A secret love is revealed when nurse Delia Busby comforts Patsy after her trauma, while Trixie's fixation with an extravagant engagement party brings conflict with Tom.

EPISODE THREE

The community is bitterly divided when future dad Tony Amos is arrested for gross indecency with another man. As homosexuality is illegal, he is compelled to undergo hormone treatment, while his young wife Marie is shunned. Shelagh races against time to halt an outbreak of dysentery and Nurse Crane's pursuit of a pregnant patient reveals a destitute family subsisting in appalling conditions in a local hostel. Tony's attempted suicide brings reconciliation, while Phyllis's fighting spirit helps rehouse the struggling family and pricks the conscience of the local council.

EPISODE FOUR

Sister Winifred cares for a pregnant prostitute suffering from syphilis and is inspired to embark on a safe sex campaign for local sex workers. Barbara tends to an expectant mother whose husband insists on a male heir to inherit his business. Sister Monica Joan finds new purpose when circumstances demand her assistance in a birth. A row with Tom over a move to a new parish leads to a break in Trixie's engagement – exposing her alcohol problem and forcing an exhausted Barbara to take up the slack.

EPISODE FIVE

An overworked Dr Turner misdiagnoses the fractured bones of a newborn infant as suspected physical abuse and the child is removed from its devout parents. When he later realises that the child has a rare bone disease, guilt over the parents' treatment leads him to a nervous collapse. Cynthia returns as Sister Mary Cynthia and Barbara helps a Sylheti mother who can only communicate in English through her young son. When her life is endangered by diphtheria, Dr Turner's timely intervention saves the day and, with Shelagh's support, he makes a recovery.

EPISODE SIX

Sister Evangelina returns with a bang; Patsy organises a square dance in aid of the Cubs and Fred plucks up the courage to ask shopkeeper Violet Gee to attend. Phyllis attends to a teenager with diabetes who falls pregnant. Dr Turner advises termination due to the complications the diabetes can cause. Rather than lose her baby, she runs away with her boyfriend, placing her life in danger. Sister Mary Cynthia cares for an expectant mother and daughter in an Irish traveller camp facing eviction and bears witness to life's beginning, and its end, in that tight-knit community.

EPISODE SEVEN

Two former school friends give birth at the maternity home on the same day. When a fire breaks out, Sister Evangelina accidentally switches the babies in the evacuation. After the mistake is revealed, there's agonised guilt for her and complex emotions for the parents. Old Gert and Tommy Mills, inseparable since the war, are torn apart when Gert is diagnosed with cancer. Fred proposes to Violet, while Patsy and Delia are determined they'll find a way to be together. Trixie's addiction worsens and the discovery of an old photograph makes Timothy Turner reflect on the loss of his mother, and his place in the new Turner family.

EPISODE EIGHT

Trixie helps a new mother who is deaf, while Delia goes flat hunting with Patsy. Fred's daughter Marlene sabotages his wedding plans with Violet but, with Chummy's help, the couple are reunited and marry. Disaster strikes when Delia is involved in a serious accident and a head injury leaves her unable to recognise Patsy. Barbara cares for a patient whose severe vomiting turns out to be the serious condition hyperemesis gravidarum. Dr Turner is delighted to treat her with a revolutionary new drug – thalidomide. Trixie finally admits she is an alcoholic and joins a support group with the help of Sister Mary Cynthia.

CHRISTMAS 1960

The BBC televise a carol service from Poplar but a measles outbreak jeopardises Shelagh's choir plans. There's pain for Iris Willens as her niece's twin birth brings back memories of losing her own child. Sister Monica Joan's sudden illness brings confusion and she goes missing from the convent, leading to a desperate search by the community. On a bus trip to see the West End Christmas lights, Patsy encounters a recovering Delia, her memory returning. The pair rekindle their feelings. Sister Monica Joan is found at her childhood home and is reunited with the Nonnatuns, while Iris's sudden back pain is found to be an undiagnosed pregnancy and she gives birth to a beautiful new daughter.

THE WOMEN IN
MY LIFE

Stephen McGann

Dr Turner

Series Four marked the arrival of women who helped to turn our drama from the hit it had been into the enduring success it was to become. The end of Series Three saw the departure of midwife Jenny Lee – the character who narrated the original books, played by the wonderful Jess Raine. Although our drama had long since moved on from that original source material, there was still some surprise that we felt able to continue without Jenny's direct involvement in the stories. But that assumed *Call the Midwife* was a drama which depended, like other TV shows, on a pivotal central character. Behind the scenes, however, there was quiet confidence that Jenny's departure would give added dramatic space to the other characters in the story.

They were right. Our hit fourth series would confirm the arrival of *Call the Midwife* as the fully-fledged ensemble drama it had always really been. Our new female arrivals in 2014 blended perfectly with those women who'd made our show famous – and the results would feel like the sixties decade we'd moved into. Fresh-faced. Forward-looking. Newly confident.

The single most important new face to arrive that year was producer,

145

and all-round queen of *Call the Midwife*, Annie Tricklebank. Our founding producer Hugh Warren had moved on and we were looking for someone who could provide long-term stability and vision for the show he'd established. We struck gold. Annie is one of British television's most experienced and talented producers, and combines this with enormous goodwill and kindness. She cares passionately for the people she works with and the drama she makes. She is the embodiment of the caring spirit of *Call the Midwife*. When Annie came on board as captain, we knew the ship was in the best hands.

That wasn't all. Two women joined our cast who were to become central characters in the *Call the Midwife* story. The first was the brilliant, clever, hilarious Charlotte Ritchie, who played Nurse Barbara Gilbert. Charlotte had already established her reputation in music, drama and comedy, yet her intelligence and sensitivity gave us something much more. Her chaotic arrival at Nonnatus House in episode one – her underwear stolen by dogs, her superfluous bananas requisitioned by Sister Monica Joan – remains one of my favourite *Call the Midwife* moments. She immediately hit it off with cast members Helen George and Emerald Fennell, and memories of this time are mostly of me giggling at the three of them when I should have been working! One night I found Helen and Emerald persuading Charlotte to venture up into the creepy Barrow Hills attic alone, *Blair Witch* style, to hunt for the ghost that Helen was convinced haunted the place! Their infectious wit filled our set and fed into those funny and tender midwife bedroom gatherings in Series Four. Our midwives felt like a genuine group of friends and colleagues because they really were.

The second cast member to join us was the legendary Phyllis Crane, played by Linda Bassett. Can you believe that there had ever been a *Call the Midwife* without Nurse Crane? Such was the impact this amazing woman made. Linda is one of the finest British character actors around. She is a tireless professional who weaves the tiniest details into her performance. From her no-nonsense arrival in episode two, she immediately captured those redemptive contrasts in human nature that *Call the Midwife* loves to highlight: officious and abrasive one minute but tender and wise the next. From driving the whole of Nonnatus House mad on her arrival, she ends episode two comforting a distraught Barbara after a traumatic birth. Phyllis reminds us that good people can be difficult, and difficult people can be capable of real goodness. We all know a Phyllis and, if we're honest, we recognise parts of her in ourselves.

Linda's arrival further bolstered an already unique quality in *Call the Midwife* – one of the secret weapons behind its success – an amazing cast of mature women. *Call the Midwife* has given wonderful roles to so many young actors but an essential anchor for those performances is the talent and wisdom of the older women in Nonnatus House, played by actors with huge gravitas and experience, but with inspiring humility.

To be on the same set with acting giants like Jenny Agutter, Pam Ferris and Judy Parfitt is quite an intimidating experience! Between them, these women have clocked up more screen time than the rest of

us could ever dream of and yet they remain unfailingly supportive and kind. Jenny is humble, smart, deeply generous and graceful, and the most wonderful friend and colleague one could have. As Sister Julienne, she has to hold the entire community together, yet still allow those moments of private vulnerability to show through. Julienne's heart-breaking encounter with an old flame in episode two is a masterclass of restrained passion and intelligence.

Our older stars were always there to support the younger actors in their work and, in Series Four, I witnessed the very deep respect that our younger stars had for their experienced colleagues. *Call the Midwife* had become a hit drama starring women of all ages – women who nurtured and celebrated each other's talents and were fully able to express their own. It was beautiful to watch but sobering to reflect that there was barely any other drama on TV like it – where a woman could be more than a murder victim or eye candy. *Call the Midwife* was single-handedly smashing barriers in women's drama representation and our huge success was sending a message that I think TV on the whole still has trouble processing.

Drama needs women. And women make really great drama.

In 2014, these were the women in my life. The women who ran the show, wrote the show and worked alongside me to make the show. These were the friends and colleagues who made me laugh, whose performances made me cry and whose wise heads made me think. To be a man working among these brilliant women in 2014 was to feel part of an important and pioneering workplace. A place where anyone, male or female, could feel they were fully supported and valued.

That, beyond any individual, remains the true heart of *Call the Midwife*.

NEW ARRIVALS

Charlotte Ritchie

Barbara Gilbert

I had to do a self-tape audition at home and after that I got a re-call to meet the director and producer, Juliet May and Annie Tricklebank. In the meantime, Heidi sent round this two-page monologue for Barbara that was about her folding up sheets for the laundry and the sheets smelling of chip fat and reminding Barbara of her life going down to the docks with her father, who was a vicar, when he was doing his rounds. I remember thinking, 'Wow, the level of thought that's gone into this character' – it was remarkable. Before that, I'd watched the programme with my mum and I'd actually said to her, 'What I wouldn't give to be in a show like this,' and then it happened! Getting that part was the best thing ever and it was such an honour to come into the series at almost the same time as Linda Bassett. The way that friendship between Barbara and Phyllis grew and the dynamic between the two characters was wonderful. It was a joy to play being mortified about sharing a bedroom and having to get undressed in front of this brusque midwife, who even went as far as putting a tape down the middle of the bedside table to mark out which side belonged to whom! Then there were the bedroom scenes with the girls, which were absolute magic. It's what I imagined boarding school must feel like, with Trixie and Delia and Patsy mucking in together, then Phyllis coming in every now and again, with her rollers in, and Sister Winifred being a nun but rather wishing she could be in with the gang.

Learning how to use the medical kit was quite challenging. Whenever we were in the clinical room where we packed our bags we had to remember the continuity. If you'd put the spatula in and then the bandages or the other way around, for some reason we'd always lose it. We'd forget our lines or start laughing hysterically – then of course we'd have to do it all again, unpack the bag and go back in. It was impossible!

Barbara was so green and gauche but she knew what she wanted. I recognise a lot of my younger self in her but she's more self-assured in some ways and it's always good to explore characteristics that you don't have. Some things didn't require much acting, like not wanting to wear a leotard and tights for Trixie's Keep Fit classes. Then we had Phyllis in Nurse Crane mode talking about American tan tights and how pulling them all the way up was going to cause all sorts of crotch problems for women. There was a brilliant bit when Barbara comes rushing in late from a difficult delivery to get ready for her first proper date with Tom and says despairingly, 'Oh gosh, I smell of sweat and amniotic fluid' – and Phyllis has laid her clothes out ready on the bed for her and hands her a washbag and towel and shoos her off to the bathroom.

Linda Bassett

Phyllis Crane

She's fiercely correct and disciplined but there is more to her than that. Heidi created her and I really enjoy playing her. I appreciate what Heidi writes for the character; there's always a touch of humour, a little twist of wit, even if she's just reading out a list of medical supplies. Her first

words to Barbara were a reprimand: 'When I was in training, we were taught to say "Good morning" or "Good afternoon", "Hello" would not have been permitted'. She was born in 1900 so she does come from a different generation to the youngsters, and she's convinced that when she's telling them off it's for their own good and they should be grateful! She thinks she's doing them a favour, teaching them the right way to do things – even though she's often just letting off steam. There was a little moment with Trixie who comes in and says, 'Might I ask your advice?', and Phyllis says, 'Of course – always ready to give advice, wanted or otherwise'. So she has a tiny bit of self-knowledge! And she may be strict and prickly with her colleagues but never with the patients. She's kind and even tender with them.

Phyllis lost her first love who was killed in the last year of the First World War. She lost her great love in the Second World War. She is wary of committing herself and identifies herself as a Useful Spinster.

I was surprised when I found in the script that she regularly does Canadian Air Force exercises. I've been doing them on and off for years. I'm not a good advert for them but they are a great way to exercise. No need for any fancy equipment – just yourself and a floor.

Phyllis reminds me of many of my own schoolteachers. They were great women, dedicated to girls' education. They could be fearsome but not too proud to sometimes act the fool and lark about.

LOVE TRIANGLE

Charlotte Ritchie

Barbara Gilbert

There was a very subtle dynamic between the three characters of Trixie, Tom and Barbara. I found it hard because I'd watched the romance blossom between Trixie and Tom as a fan and I really wanted them to be happy. When I learnt that Barbara was going to get involved with Tom I thought, 'Are you sure?' Barbara's absolutely not a homewrecker and it made for a rare bit of conflict between the midwives. That was a strange, jarring thing because it was in every other way so strongly about sisterhood. But then the whole story developed really beautifully, allowing for a lot of generous letting go and forgiveness. Trixie is such a stoical character, constantly picking herself up again and carrying on – brilliantly played by Helen.

Helen George

Trixie Franklin

What is very special about *Call the Midwife* is that there's a feeling of being trusted with the material and that Heidi writes with our voices in mind. Her writing isn't easy to learn but it's so ingrained in me – the muscularity of the way she moves through a sentence. Trixie's vulnerability is revealed along with her strength and confidence. She was incredibly clear-sighted about her relationship with Tom. It wasn't working and she recognised that – she didn't try to flog a dead horse. She went, right, no, I'm not settling for an unhappy relationship. That's a powerful asset – that certainty allied with sensibility.

Jack Ashton

Tom Hereward

It was rather extraordinary to be called in to audition for the role of Tom. I don't think I'd ever have thought of going up for it because I'd always played more laddish characters. The idea of being a vicar wasn't really on the cards but I was intrigued, and I knew how popular the show was. Having the name Ashton is quite useful because auditions are invariably done in alphabetical order so you're not turning up in a room where they've been auditioning all day and everyone just wants to go home – you're usually met with a certain amount of enthusiasm. But on this occasion, being A and going in early didn't help because I was really disappointed with the way I performed. When I'd finished they just said, 'Thank you very much' – no notes, no response, no, 'Could you just try it like this?' – and when I left, as the door closed behind me, they all burst out laughing. I was a bit devastated. So I rang my agent and told her that it hadn't gone too well and that I'd really like to have another go as I thought I could do better. She said, 'We should hang on. Let's just see what they have to say first.' And I was offered the part! Two episodes at first, with a view to there possibly being more. That 'view' lasted for five years altogether – and I never found out what they were all laughing about but it couldn't have been too negative. I like to think it was because I was the first guy in and they thought they didn't need to see anyone else. You never know!

Joining such a strong ensemble cast, particularly with so many women, so many legendary actresses, was quite daunting. My first day was on location, at a prison in Lincoln. I was confident and excited until I stepped into the prison and all of a sudden my confidence left me and the lines just went. I was face to face with Jenny Agutter and she's such a pro – she could see that I was quaking. The camera was on her, over my shoulder, and we did a line run and I must have said about three words in the right place. She just said, very quietly, 'Don't worry, the camera's on me, say whatever you want' – I've loved her ever since that day.

The Trixie and Tom story started before we were Jack and Helen in real life. We'd never met before *Call the Midwife* and we became really good friends. Then, as soon as I married Barbara in the show, Helen and I started going out together. I have the fondest memories of that time – it was Tom and Trixie against the world and the story was so set for them to make it but their acceptance of it not being right was beautifully done. When people really care about one another they can be generous – they had to watch each other move away. And there was an inevitability about Tom and Barbara. She was the daughter of a reverend; they were such a good fit.

SHOULDER TO SHOULDER

Victoria Yeates

Sister Winifred

I think my favourite thing about being an actor is that you mix with such a wide age range and become friends with people you wouldn't otherwise come into contact with. The *Call the Midwife* cast is fantastic – the kind of people you dream of working with. Some of them were people I'd watched on television when I was a teenager thinking how much I'd love to be doing what they were doing, to be somewhere, anywhere near as good as them. And then I found myself sitting round that table in Nonnatus House with some of those very women. I just soaked it up – there was so much to learn from them, about how to act on set, how to break down a scene, how to be collaborative. Pam Ferris was wonderful at that. And performers' etiquette – turning your phone off, being aware of what the crew are doing. I also learnt from her and the others how to look after your character. You get lots of different directors on a long-running show so you need to know exactly who your character is; it's a sort of self-protection. They taught us how to hold onto that. And of course, Heidi looks after the story and keeps a consistency running through it. There were days when I just couldn't wait to get to work because of the people and the supportive company feeling.

Everyone was so generous and encouraging. It's unusual to have so many women, in front of the camera and behind it, and there really was no sense of competition – everybody wanted everybody else to have their moment to shine.

Learning to drive was a wonderfully funny storyline – me and Linda Bassett in a car together! When I first got the part I thought it would be really interesting to play someone who's lovely but slightly annoying. I like that contradiction. We're all a mass of contradictions and it's important to recognise that you can love people but be irritated by them as well. Sister Winifred is sweet and bubbly but you saw more of her inner strength towards the end when she fought to stay at the children's home, saying, 'No, this is where I should be.' She was a teacher and she's got that essence that children open up to, that big smile.

Bryony Hannah

Sister Mary Cynthia

I was on the show for six years so, as a character and as myself, I had six years of shared experience with those women. By the end, we knew each other almost as well as the real women would have done. And I had the strange experience of switching over. Cynthia became a postulant and then joined the religious Order as Sister Mary Cynthia so I had to move places at the table and sit on the other side – it felt very strange. So much happens round that table and when I watched my younger colleagues having fun, wearing wonderful clothes, it felt very real, being different, having changed, wearing a different costume.

At the start, we were all finding our feet – for Jess, Helen and me it was our first major television work. That forged our friendship and it was so special. Doing photoshoots, filming long hours – then life happens alongside it and you grow and change and it can't help but affect your character. I'm amazed it's been ten years! I signed up for one series and they were hoping they might do a second but nobody really knew.

Laura Main

Shelagh Turner

I love the relationship between Shelagh and Sister Julienne – that one got named #Shulienne on Twitter! Jenny and I lived quite near each other so we'd quite often get put in the same car for transport, so it wasn't just the time we spent on set but travelling to and from work together. That was mirrored on screen – she's a confidante, a friend and a mentor. Just occasionally on the show it's the other way around and Sister Julienne needs support from Shelagh, who's become quite bossy over the years.

BACKGROUND RESEARCH

Heidi Thomas

Writer and executive producer

Each series of *Call the Midwife* covers one calendar year and the very first series was set in 1957. As it became evident that the show was a success and would be recommissioned, when we finish filming one series, my mind is already turning to the next. We usually know by then if any actors aren't rejoining us and I always look at the characters first and how their stories might develop.

From Series Two onwards, Jennifer Worth's books were no longer providing the bulk of the material so I had to look to other sources for material and inspiration. An invaluable source is the Wellcome Trust archive library, which houses, for example, the official reports from the medical officer for Poplar for each year. These are wonderfully comprehensive reports and they include narrative passages on housing, which was a huge thing in the 1960s, with tenements being demolished and tower blocks going up. There were updates on what was happening about the rats, which were a particular problem around bombsites, and about fleas and bedbugs.

Statistics give me ideas about medical content and birth content. I noticed very early on – and this informed much of my thinking about the morality of the world in which *Call the Midwife* is set – that all the statistics about birth have two entries, under the headings of legitimate or illegitimate babies. In other words, whether the mother was married was a matter of medical record, which shows how the notion of a child being born out of wedlock was so entrenched. In the East End in the late 1950s, one in ten babies was born to an unmarried mother. That opened up a whole world of narrative and drama. A boyfriend who wouldn't step up to the plate and propose marriage; the terrible predicament of a pregnant, unmarried woman.

There are records of measles epidemics, or an outbreak of polio, all tied specifically to moments in history. In the most recent series, we've reached 1967 and vaccinations are starting to happen. Measles is still around but polio has been pretty much eradicated and there's far less TB. There's talk about cervical cytology – smear tests – and it was up to a GP like Dr Turner to decide whether to add it to what his surgery offers.

I look at Hansard as well, for details of specific parliamentary debates. In Series Ten, for example, the legalisation of abortion is coming nearer and nearer so I looked up the debates about that.

STORYTELLING
WITH A PURPOSE

Annie Tricklebank

Producer, Series 4–10

It's unusual to work together with the same team for so long, and along the way we've developed a kind of shorthand, as well as an increasing respect for each other. In my job, you've got to entertain the people who are going to watch what you've made and along the way you've got to make it interesting. If you can put those two things together successfully it can become quite important – your storytelling has a purpose to it; it becomes more than just entertainment. I've spoken to so many people who watch *Call the Midwife* and it's not just that the audience is hugely diverse – they appreciate that our storytelling is hugely diverse. Because we've had Heidi writing from the beginning, the thread of the story never frays. She's constantly picking up new stories and following up ideas but she never forgets the essential imperative to make all the characters believable. You believe in their stories and you believe in them.

It avoids nostalgia; it's painful; it's honest and it's gritty. There's always something that touches the heart, that we can all empathise with. I've lost count of the number of times people have said to me, 'That happened to me,' or to their mother or grandmother. It might be

racism, deafness, spina bifida, blindness, thalidomide, debt, homophobia – basically, the problems that people encountered in the 1950s are problems we still have today. *Call the Midwife* pulls all those things together, shows them, says, 'Look, this is what happened to this person and this is how they dealt with it.' It may have taken place in 1959 or 1964 but a lot of those things are still happening and what we can do is say, 'Please watch, please take note, we can still do something about this.'

THE POWER
OF LOVE

Kate Lamb
Delia Busby

Delia comes into the series a bit sideways in a way – she's not one of the Nonnatus gang, although she does get to move in there eventually. She'd managed to get away from home in order to train as a nurse in London but her mother is incredibly overbearing and controlling and won't let go. Maxine Evans played her and she was amazing – she embodied all that. The joy and strength of Heidi's writing is marvellous, and the way she built the story of Delia and Patsy's relationship was so subtle. I'm proud of being part of that because of the way it was handled, the delicacy of the writing that enabled it to come into people's living rooms on a Sunday night. For girls and young women to be able to see that lovely friendship and to be rooting for it because those two people love each other. It also made it possible to see another side of Patsy – she's so startlingly efficient and competent but with Delia she can open up and be happy, softer.

I never got to do a delivery on camera but I did have to handle one on the telephone. It was fantastic but completely bonkers – just a huge monologue, really, having to learn pages of talking to no one, pretending there was someone giving birth at the other end. It was great for Delia to discover that she could manage that. When she had a bike accident and lost her memory I remember thinking, 'My twelve-year-old self would be very happy with this turn of events – I've got myself a part in a very popular BBC drama and I've got amnesia!'

Playing a proper Welsh character was lovely. From the age of around sixteen or maybe even younger I'd wanted to be an actress but at the time, the only Welsh voice I'd heard on screen was Rhys Ifans in *Notting Hill*. It seemed to me then that Welsh people were presented as the joke – they were the stupid, silly, gross ones. So I edged away from it and worked incredibly hard to lose the accent so my voice was neutral. I've ended up feeling a bit disloyal so it was great when playing Delia showed me that you can be a fully rounded, beautiful human being and have a Welsh accent. It was a joy to do that.

Emerald Fennell

Patsy Mount

It seems absurd that it was unusual to show a relationship between two women, but *Call the Midwife* is family viewing and it was still quite out there at the time. It was so beautifully done – finely drawn, an integral part of the story. We got an extraordinary response, from young women and girls who were watching with their parents, their grandparents, and found that it started a conversation. It was just there, presented without fuss – a lovely, happy relationship. There was very little angst about it, apart from Delia's accident and amnesia, which was typically clever of Heidi's writing – rather than having a cumbersome speech to explain the social pressures of the time, she made it a gripping way of showing how few rights you had. Patsy was suddenly confronted with not being told anything, having no official place in Delia's life, not even being allowed to visit.

When I think of why the programme is so popular, apart from delicious babies, I think it's because you see a group of women who all get on with each other, who are in functioning relationships, who know their worth. It shows women's friendships that are like the ones we really have, not adversarial, bullying or cruel. In the main we like each other, we support each other, we don't fall out and scream all the time – that's not how we live, and it's not mushy and cosy, but it is warm and innately female. Women deal with adversity with a lot of stoicism and grace and very few histrionics.

SERIES FIVE

1961

EPISODE ONE

Nonnatus House is shocked when local mum Rhoda Mullucks gives birth to a daughter, Susan, with severe and unexplained physical deformities. Rhoda won't abandon Susan but Bernie, her husband, struggles to come to terms with the harsh realities. Trixie finds new purpose in running a Keep Fit class for local women – but the suffering of an older participant highlights the shame still blighting discussion of women's health. Tom recruits Barbara's help in organising the Easter Parade; Delia returns to Nonnatus House and Patsy, and unauthorised photos of the midwives in a local paper lands Trixie in trouble with Sister Julienne.

EPISODE TWO

Barbara is concerned about expectant mother Stella Beckett's well-being, as her dockworker husband Johnny seems unable to find work. When Johnny's apparent idleness turns out to be leukaemia, Barbara and the team race to induce Stella's baby so that Johnny might see it before he dies. Phyllis has her hopes raised when she meets a widower at her new Spanish class but is humiliated when his true circumstances are revealed. And when Sister Evangelina's dogmatism about breastfeeding puts a struggling mother and baby in danger, her remorse leads her to a period of reflection at a silent Order.

EPISODE THREE

When a local outbreak of deadly typhoid impacts on a close-knit family and its matriarch, it brings back bad memories for Patsy and impacts on her relationship with Delia. Sister Winifred faces a personal dilemma when a local schoolteacher becomes pregnant by a married man and is forced out of her job and accommodation. When the desperate woman attempts an abortion, Sister Winifred is forced to consider the role her own prejudices played. Meanwhile, Barbara agrees to go to dinner with Tom but is wracked with worry about how Trixie will react.

EPISODE FOUR

Sister Julienne is seconded to St Cuthbert's Hospital and is impressed by the medical advances there. But when Ruby Cottingham's baby is born with terrible deformities, the shocking manner of the child's death brings a moral crisis and the number of incidences of children born this way poses disturbing questions for Dr Turner and Shelagh. Meanwhile, Ian Bulmer's dreams of university are shattered when his girlfriend Linda Lanyard falls pregnant and family demands override his plans. Tom and Trixie help the couple to avert disaster and find a better future, while Trixie encourages Tom and Barbara to seek a future of their own.

EPISODE FIVE

After a traumatic birth at home alone, Roseanne Dawley feels haunted by her past and unable to embrace motherhood with her loving husband. She flees back to her old prostitute's life but, with Nurse Crane's support, is reconciled with her family and the future she deserves. Dr Turner and Shelagh organise a chest clinic for their patients but Timothy forces them to address the dangers in their own smoking.

When Violet is laid low with back trouble she entrusts Fred with the running of her shop, with less than perfect results. Yet she comes to value Fred's good intentions more than the scorn of her customers.

EPISODE SIX

When a sex worker is violently attacked, Tom and Barbara are frustrated by the lack of police help. After a young mother is also assaulted, a criminal pattern becomes clear. An exhausted Dr Turner is persuaded to take a camping holiday with his family but the trip proves a washout and the Turners end up checking into a nearby hotel. There's danger when a mother attempts to deliver her unmarried daughter's baby herself and pass it off as her own. And there's horror when Sister Mary Cynthia becomes the attacker's next victim and must summon the courage to help in his capture.

EPISODE SEVEN

The new contraceptive pill is announced and Dr Turner and Shelagh eagerly discuss its benefits with the Nonnatuns but Sister Julienne fears the moral implications. There's embarrassment when Tom and Barbara's passion rubs off on the Nonnatus wall, while Patsy and Sister Winifred visit Daisy Blacker, a pregnant mum from the barge community who's determined to have her baby on board without help. When a violent storm strikes Poplar, Nurse Crane rescues a mother with pre-eclampsia and helps her young husband to assume his new life responsibilities. Patsy attends Daisy's storm-ridden barge delivery

and the unique experience encourages her to find a place to celebrate her own identity with Delia.

EPISODE EIGHT

There's horror at Nonnatus House when Distaval, the thalidomide drug prescribed by Dr Turner, is revealed to have caused the birth deformities in the district. A desperate race is on to retrieve the drug from pregnant patients, while it falls to the team to tell those women already affected, Rhoda and Ruby, the harsh truth. An unmarried couple are keen to arrange a hasty wedding with Tom before the imminent birth of their child but the two events end up as one. And tragedy strikes when Sister Evangelina dies suddenly at the convent. Her moving community funeral marks the climax to the series.

CHRISTMAS 1961

The Nonnatuns' Christmas plans are set aside when the team travels to South Africa to assist a rural mission hospital threatened with closure. The team are shaken and exhilarated by the challenges they face: a polio immunisation programme, life-saving trips to challenging locations, a caesarean operation by candlelight. As the clinic's capable doctor falls dangerously ill, they must find a way to soften the heart of a local land-owner and secure access to the water supply that will save the clinic's future. Through their efforts to save Hope Clinic and the lives of the people who use it, their own lives are changed for ever.

SPRING 2015

Stephen McGann

Dr Turner

'She's here. Susan. Would you like to see her?'

I remember the way Stella said it. Hesitant. Respectful. Like asking if I'd like to pay my respects at someone's coffin.

I'm in the make-up chair at Longcross. Make-up supervisor Stella O'Farrell is cutting my hair – turning my overgrown 2015 mess into Dr Turner's sixties trim. We've been talking about the forthcoming storyline in Series Five. There's only one topic of conversation. Thalidomide.

I was born in 1963 so those children were older than me by a few years. But I remember seeing one or two of those kids playing in the Liverpool streets where I grew up. I would stare at their little limbless bodies with an infant's brutal fascination. My mother would push me on, her small shudder signalling a parent's empathetic horror. That cold sniper's bullet, dodged by blind luck. That terrible wound that couldn't heal.

Heidi always knew what 1961 would bring for *Call the Midwife* if we ever reached Series Five. It rolled in slowly, like a storm on the horizon, as each new series was commissioned. Something any medical drama set in 1961 must confront. Something Heidi had no intention of avoiding.

Thalidomide. That first great pharmaceutical scandal. Post-war health's most devastating loss of innocence. Dr Turner would be directly in the line of fire as the story unfolded. At the end of Series Four, Heidi had placed a chilling reference to thalidomide as a new wonder drug that Dr Turner was delighted to dispense. When that line was spoken in the script read-through the previous year, reactions divided perfectly by age. The older half of the room gasped at the word. The younger half looked up, confused. Our society was forgetting what had happened. We were about to remind them.

Stella's job is about more than cutting the hair of middle-aged actors. She's a vital *Call the Midwife* talent – responsible for our detailed medical effects and prosthetics. If there's a seeping wound, a scar, a flesh discolouration, then it's Stella's research and artistry that brings it to life on camera. So when the technical challenges of thalidomide presented themselves, Stella played a central role.

And the challenges were profound. Thankfully, there are no more young children in our world injured by thalidomide. So if we were to represent these injuries, it had to be by a combination of computer effects, skilled prosthetic modelling and clever make-up design. The result of this combination of talents now lay in a sealed box in Stella's trailer. Baby Susan. She'd arrived from the modellers that morning. Stella hadn't yet seen the finished result.

Susan Mullucks was the character name of the infant in episode one who is born without limbs, due to her mum Rhoda being given Distaval during pregnancy. She was to be played by our most ambitious prosthetic model to date. Stella broke the seal and we both looked into the box at the beautiful thing inside. An exquisite infant made of silicone – of human weight and authentic feel – intricate veins visible on its skin and real human hair on its tiny scalp. The little hands and feet were twisted into tiny stumps on her body and a tangle of wires and handles ran from her back. *Call the Midwife* had used many prosthetic infants before, but Susan was special. The tiny hands and feet that protruded from her body were animatronic and controlled by separate hydraulic levers so that she would make lifelike movements when Laura and I filmed our emotional scenes with her.

We stared into the box for a minute without saying anything. When I looked up, there were tears brimming in Stella's eyes. I felt it too. The solemnity of it. The importance of what we were trying to do. The enormous responsibility we felt towards those who still endured it.

There are hundreds of thalidomide survivors alive today. To them, the scandal isn't just a storyline – an episode of drama to be played and broadcast. It's a daily reality. Susan wasn't based on any living person but was a carefully researched construction of typical injuries and family profile. She was the 'unknown warrior' for a multitude of real battles, standing for the courage and anguish of real mothers and the struggles of real children, and paying tribute to the real infants who didn't make it, their injuries too profound. Susan didn't belong to us. We had simply borrowed her from the people whose experiences she represented.

Filming those scenes with Susan in episode one had that same air of solemnity. Shelagh's shock at her birth and then the isolation room as we gazed into her cot, unable to believe she could survive. I remember our director, Syd Macartney, controlling the movement of her limbs as the cameras rolled. This model wasn't an inanimate thing to us. She had her character's name, like the other cast members. She was one of the team.

That episode contains my favourite ever *Call the Midwife* moment. It's the scene where Rhoda Mullucks, played brilliantly by Liz White, is first introduced to her child Susan and her injuries. Everybody leaves the room and Rhoda unwraps her baby. Her breath stops as she sees her profound deformities.

'Oh love,' she says. 'What a mess. What a mess, eh?'

We watch Rhoda draw her courage up in a quiet sniff.

'We'll sort something out. I promise. Because you're mine. *Mine.* And I'm not bailing out on you.'

It makes me cry every time. Even now, as I'm writing this.

There are many things that drama isn't. It isn't a newspaper investigation, hunting for the truth. It isn't a documentary, laying out the facts. It isn't a medical journal, presenting cold evidence and procedure. But what it can be, in those moments, is something uniquely powerful.

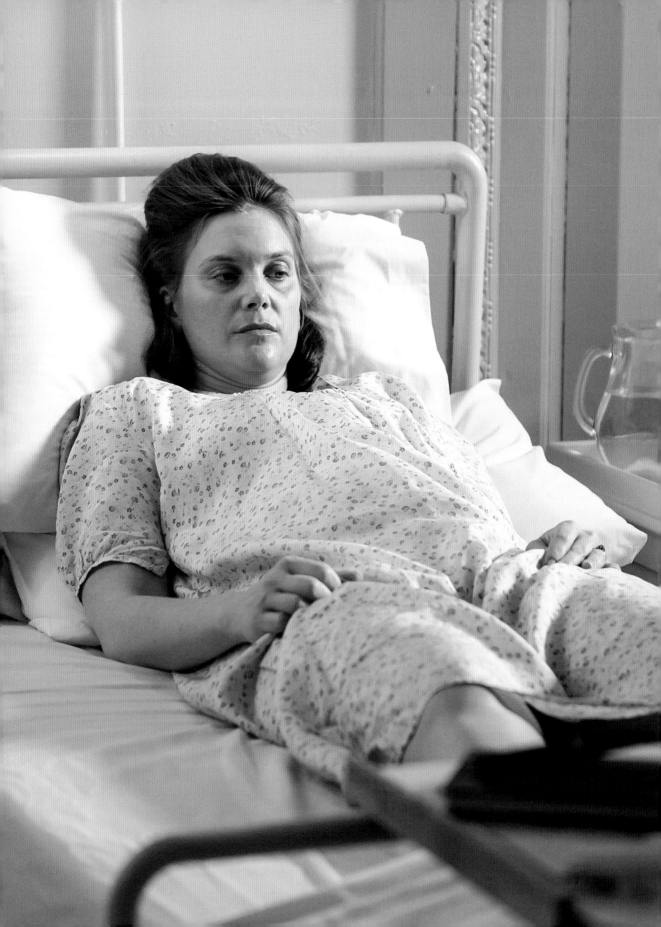

Call the Midwife took an audience of millions into that room in 1961. To a place where one of those mothers sat alone with one of those blameless children and somehow found the courage to go on. A fictional mother and child, yes, but created to speak for all of them. And to all of us.

Drama is a way for us to grasp the humanity inherent in all of life's biggest moments. A way to give voice to the silent courage of nameless people. A way to name the things we feel, and feel these things in common.

Her name was Susan. We all loved her. Because every real life she represented was worth it.

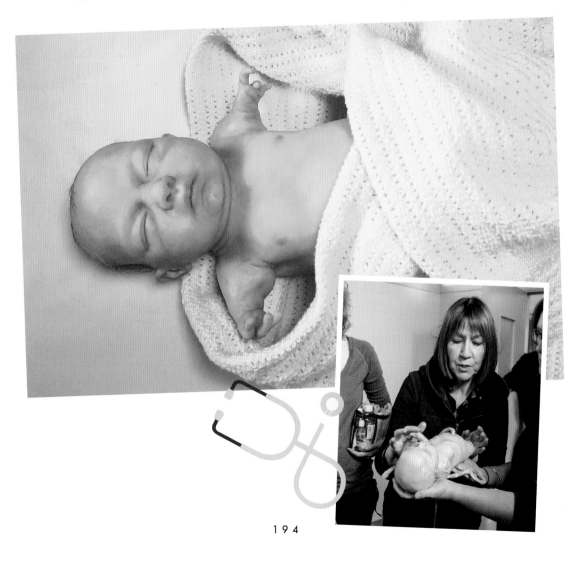

CONFRONTING THALIDOMIDE

Laura Main

Shelagh Turner

I have a vivid recollection of the build-up between Series Four and Five, knowing that the thalidomide story was coming, that there were going to be difficult and harrowing scenes. I remember how we all just really wanted to do our part in telling that story as well as we possibly could, respecting its truth. It's the storyline I always go back to, that had the biggest effect on me, wanting so much to do it justice. Something that *Call the Midwife* does so well is that whenever it takes on a complex, sensitive subject, it's done in conjunction with a charity, with experts in that field, representing the people who will be most affected by the programme and seeing the topic addressed. That was definitely the case with thalidomide, and with female genital mutilation, and many other issues.

It's so important to get these things right. These are raw, painful subjects and the BBC is putting them into people's living rooms at 8 p.m. on a Sunday evening. It makes me feel very emotional to look back on this – oh god, I sound like such an actress, but it does touch you. There's a feeling of wanting to do your bit and I've always ended up feeling proud of the finished product.

Jenny Agutter

Sister Julienne

Call the Midwife is unflinching, it's always on the edge, as in the episode where Sister Julienne finds a severely thalidomide baby that's been deliberately left to die in a hospital storeroom. She knows it's dying and she refuses to let the child die alone so she baptises it and gives it a blessing. Heidi wrote in that same blessing later on, when Sister Julienne delivers Shelagh's baby. It was a wonderful balance – a child that was dying and a child that's going to survive. We confront those things on the programme – life and death and birth and never being entirely sure. Babies always bring hope but still things can go so badly wrong.

Heidi Thomas

Writer and executive producer

Given the time frame of *Call the Midwife*, I knew from an early stage that if the series got as far as 1961, we would need to confront the scandal of thalidomide. As I am the same age as the original survivors, it was something I had been aware of since childhood. There was a boy I'd see at our local swing park who was affected in all four limbs. It was very visible and very apparent. From the outset, I knew that the story would need an extended dramatic arc and could not be confined to a single episode. We made contact with the Thalidomide Society, who hold strongly to the mantra 'Nothing About Us Without Us', and three of their members came to the Neal Street Productions office to meet us. One of them, Guy Tweedy, gave me some documents to read, correspondence between the thalidomide community and the government in their fight for financial compensation. Those papers convinced me to take up the cudgels in a campaigning way – they were so shocking that I remember looking at the bag I'd put them in to take them home and being astonished it didn't burst into flames.

I was determined to tell the story from numerous perspectives – those of the parents, the doctors, the nurses and the siblings. We were contacted by a wonderful man called Ed Freeman who was born in 1959 and is thus one of the oldest members of the thalidomide community. Ed is a fan of *Call the Midwife*, and his family originate from Stepney, in the East End. He offered us a copy of a diary written by his late father, a bus driver, when Ed was a young child. This generous gift gave me an exceptional insight into the world of thalidomide families, and Ed and I became good friends. I also got to know Rosie Moriarty-Simmonds, who is a tireless disability campaigner, born without limbs.

Creating fiction around fact makes you personally invested in those people and their stories. *Call the Midwife* is a family and the thalidomide community is like that a thousand-fold – they've shared so much. One of the things that Ed and Rosie said to me after we got to know one another was how they feel that their generation will die out and that they don't want to become a historical footnote. They want to be remembered so that the tragedy will not be repeated.

When the thalidomide story was flagged up at the end of Series Four, it was in the context of treating hyperemesis gravidarum, a complication of pregnancy that causes extreme sickness. In episode eight, Dr Turner prescribed Distaval, a sedative drug sometimes given to calm hacking coughs, not just for morning sickness. The shudder that went through social media at that point was a real reminder of how important this story was.

In Series Five, we then saw the birth of Susan, a baby with severe limb anomalies. It was crucial to me to show the experience of the mother, Rhoda Mullucks, played with such tenderness by Liz White. There was no pre-natal testing then and most women would never have seen a child like that before – it would have come as a terrible shock. In fact, many people wouldn't have been familiar with disability at all because those children were hidden away. It was a society where you were encouraged to let go of disabled children and put them into institutional care. About 50 per cent of parents of thalidomiders did that, but others brought them home, in many ways bucking the trend of that time. It took incredible bravery, facing up to profound emotional trauma and challenge.

What was interesting was how, by Series Five, we were particularly well placed to tell that story because CGI and medical prosthetics had come such a long way. We wouldn't have had those resources earlier.

Stella O'Farrell

Hair and make-up supervisor, Series 4–10

It was an exceptional challenge to produce a prosthetic model for a thalidomide baby and we did it in three stages – a newborn, then six months later and then eighteen months later. We worked with the company Millennium FX and in particular a man called Waldo Emerson. The discussions went back and forth about how each limb should look. There were so many details to be aware of and we took the greatest possible care not to do anything that could be picked up as wrong. For example, we found out that if a child whose mother had taken thalidomide was born with a digit that could be termed a thumb, an opposing digit, the child didn't get compensated.

It was very moving when some thalidomiders came to watch the filming. Heidi came onto the make-up bus with this lovely lady, Mikey Argy, and we gave her the prosthetic baby to hold. She was overcome – she'd never held a child like herself, like she had once been. It was an extraordinary experience for her.

We filmed again when Baby Susan was older and we had some bigger limbs made. Then we used green screen, with a real child's face superimposed and the prosthetic limbs fitted with animatronics so that they could move. All the models have gone to museums – one to Dr Ruth Blue at the Thalidomide Society, one to the *Call the Midwife* exhibit at Historic Dockyard Chatham and one to the National Science and Media Museum.

People often ask about babies that are seen on screen just after birth. I work very closely with Terri Coates, who's on hand for advice and is always on set with the tiny babies. I supply organic grapeseed oil and vegan 'blood' from special effects make-up suppliers, and also

Sudocrem, that's specifically for babies, mixed with a tiny bit of grease-paint to get that off-white colour for the vernix. And greasepaint again for forceps marks because it's hypoallergenic. Terri smears the make-up on herself.

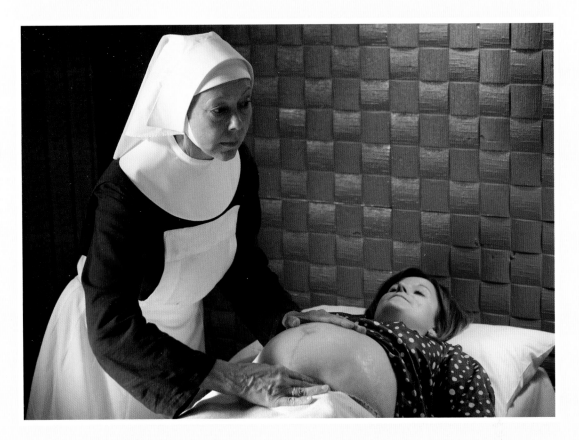

We also work closely with costume regarding pregnancy bumps. If the character is fully dressed or in a nightie then it's generally a bump made by the costume department, but if it's revealed and shown to be examined by one of the midwives then it needs to be one of our make-up bumps, made out of soft silicone and padded with foam. Vicky Voller makes those – and all the umbilical cords – and that's a crossover with the props department. It's often Terri's hands shown cutting the umbil-ical cord because she's done it so often for real and it just looks better when she does it.

Terri Coates

Midwifery advisor

I've cut hundreds of prosthetic umbilical cords over the course of the series. Once I've got two pairs of gloves on – a clear plastic pair under the rubber ones – my hands could be anybody's. No marks or blemishes or distinguishing features show. My husband's a paediatrician and he's been Dr Turner's hands a few times. The prosthetic babies are quite remarkable and the people who make them are real artists. One thing I do find disturbing is that they're so pale and cool to touch, with no muscle tone, that they feel like a dead baby. I don't get emotional about the childbirths on set but what does bring back memories is when something goes wrong – if there's a stillbirth. It's not as if it comes as a surprise or that I don't have time to prepare myself, but after forty years of clinical experience I remember cases where that's actually happened so that can be very difficult to detach from. It's very affecting and I stand there with red eyes and tissues and try not to make a noise. It gives a truth to the storytelling – we don't hold back from the difficult stories. My husband came onto the set once and somebody handed him one of the prosthetic babies. I looked at him and saw his colour drain. They're so realistic that he thought for a moment that he'd been given a dead baby to hold. I had to rush over and reassure him.

THE PAIN
BENEATH

Bryony Hannah

Sister Mary Cynthia

It's quite strange to look back on an experience that has left me with exceptionally happy memories and remember how fragile my character was and how she was put through the wringer. It was only once we had finished filming that I realised how dark it had been. Performing as someone with serious mental health issues does touch you personally – and it has to, otherwise you can't touch an audience. Of course, there's a professional discipline that comes into play but it brings a new perspective; you think of yourself differently.

When Cynthia was in a mental asylum it felt almost as if I was a guest on another show. The set was different, none of my regular colleagues were around – in some ways I suppose it helped the disconnect that she was feeling: isolated on alien territory. But my happiest times were early on, as a young midwife – those bedroom scenes, when Trixie and Jenny and Cynthia were playing Monopoly or something and I couldn't hold my drink so got a bit tipsy. Those intimate things, and the times sitting around the table at Nonnatus House, drinking endless cups of tea, or having quiet chats with people on the little journeys, walking to and from the car park where we were based. I loved it.

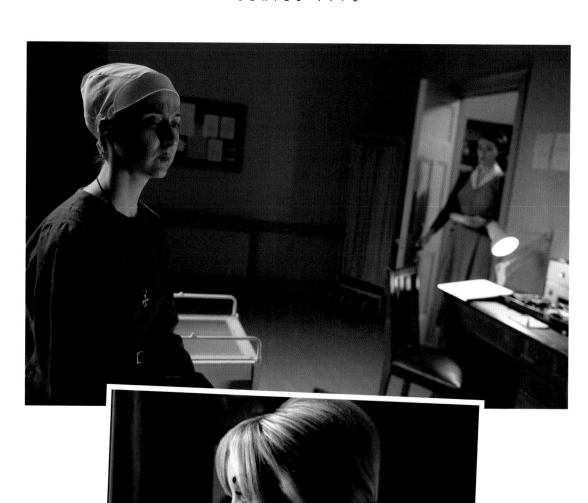

Helen George

Trixie Franklin

There was a turning point for Trixie in Series Three when she unburdened herself to Jenny about her father and his alcoholism and trauma after the war. It was the first time you got a real sense of her and from that moment there was licence to go behind the façade with Trixie, to show her vulnerability and what she's like when the bedroom door shuts, which is as much a part of her as her strength and confidence.

The topic of addiction within the medical profession is an important one, and became even more so during the pandemic, and it needs to be talked about. It was important for it to be Trixie, who had been seen as something of a good-time girl but was struggling with her own demons. I hadn't seen it coming but when I learnt about it I thought, 'Of course, that makes sense.' There was a lot of responsibility to deliver that story truthfully but I didn't want to research it into the ground. I checked out some AA meetings on YouTube that were very helpful. Trixie's experience was deeply private and had no obvious pattern. It had always been a quiet alcoholism, a dependency to help her get through – she was never going to be screaming drunk and out of control at 3 o'clock in the morning.

Her relationship with Sister Julienne is pivotal and I love those encounters they have in her office. It's a pretty appalling thing for a midwife, a professional with huge responsibilities, to be found to be drinking on the job. Sister Julienne gives her unstinting strength and support while recognising all her flaws. She believes in her and inspires her. And as an actress I find that intriguing because there's a conflict between the modern nursing world and the more traditional nuns' world. Sister Julienne has to expand her understanding and both characters are pushed to explore their own beliefs and thoughts.

GROWING UP ON SET

Max Macmillan

Timothy Turner

I was eleven when I started, though I was playing a few years younger than that. The series has been a major part of my life for a long time and people on set have become like a second family, especially members of the crew who've been around since the beginning. It's such a familiar, friendly, comfortable place to work and I've been able to experience working in a professional way in a professional environment. I haven't really had stage fright. If I get nervous I look around and see that people are just getting the job done and if I can get into that mindset, realising how unimportant I am in the grand scheme of things, I can switch off my brain to a certain extent and just be a cog in the machine.

I think I was pretty much a blank slate when I started. People have said that I looked a bit like Stephen McGann so that was useful as he plays my dad. He knew how much I was into music because he is as well and he asks a lot of questions. So music has sneaked in and Heidi's written in a bit of piano playing for me and some intentionally bad violin. There's always a lot of waiting around in between takes and it can be quite slow and dull at times but then you find yourself in the middle of a great scene, like when the Turners went camping and it rained the entire time. We had a rain machine and Stephen and I had to do this big comedy tent-fail thing. Some of the Cub Scout scenes were quite funny as well – it seems so long ago now. I remember the year I was finally allowed to wear long trousers. That was quite a moment!

It might sound callous but I had a really good time staggering about in leg irons for the polio story. There wasn't much technique to the acting – you wear them and they do the job for you! At the time I was fascinated by the callipers, and for someone who was too young to be really tuned into the more emotional side of the story, it was a lot of fun having the dramatic, nearly dying scenes, being in an iron lung. A couple of years later I might have been a bit paranoid about taking on such an important storyline. As I've got older I have a tendency to over-think things but back then it was just 'Bring it on!'

What I'm really interested in now is directing and I had the most incredible opportunity to learn on the job. Whenever I could, I'd go up to members of various departments and ask them what things are and what they do, trying to learn useful tricks for the no-budget stuff I get to do now I'm at uni. Annie Tricklebank arranged for me to do two weeks of shadowing with director Noreen Kershaw, and she was the best mentor I could possibly have hoped for. She's a wonderful director – honest and engaging and really generous. It was an incredible experience and I took pages and pages of notes. It made me realise how much you miss as an actor, how much you don't see of the preparations and technical work. Out of all the time spent on set, actors are probably there for 50 per cent of the time.

BETWEEN THE LINES

Pam Ferris

Sister Evangelina

There's a sort of etiquette about how to behave on set. If you've been in the business a long time, as I have, you know how difficult the technicians' work is, how complex. If you're new to it, you can think that it's just about you and your performance; it's easy to think that everything else happens almost by magic. When I started filming, there were no walkie-talkies or mics on the mouth for people to communicate with each other. Camera crew would have to shout across the room – 'Up an inch, down an inch' – so you heard the preparations and slowly you'd begin to understand it, to tune in and know from the way they were talking whether they were five minutes off a take or ten minutes. They can talk quietly to each other now, so you're unaware of all that.

If there's a bunch of actors on set and we're between takes it's important not to get loud and turn it into a cocktail party – that makes it really hard for the crew. I like to watch them and work out whether it's likely to be a long or a short pause, then you're ready when you're required to be. I was pleased that Victoria Yeates [who plays Sister Winifred] was so interested; I'd spend time with her pointing out different crew members and what they were doing. It was good to get a chance to explain, 'That's the grip, making sure that camera shot goes seamlessly.' That sort of thing.

Call the Midwife has a tight schedule with no rehearsal time built in, but if you have some experience you know that lighting time is always necessary so if you're lucky, you can walk into a corner with someone and discuss the scene, then you're right back in and you have to be ready. You're not just portraying a character, you're creating a scene and a dramatic tension with other characters. That takes time to establish so sometimes you have to fight for a little space on a really fast shoot.

In the acting profession you never completely say goodbye to people because you can find yourself working with them again, in another context. Linda Bassett and I had known each other for years, and I knew Judy Parfitt but we became really good mates. It was marvellous that she and I played two characters who were so difficult, with Jenny Agutter as Sister Julienne in charge, hoping they could work together and knock the corners off each other. I enjoyed that relationship on and off screen.

Judy Parfitt

Sister Monica Joan

Sister Monica Joan's endless teasing of Sister Evangelina was glorious, but the two women had a real affection for each other underneath. It was such a genius idea of Heidi's to write in that moment at Sister Evangelina's funeral when Sister Monica Joan goes out with her shoes and puts them on the coffin. I always thought that was the most brilliant thing; it said so much. The shoes take on the character of a person.

SERIES SIX

1962

EPISODE ONE

The midwives return home from South Africa to discover that stern Sister Ursula is now in charge of Nonnatus House with Sister Julienne relegated to lesser duties. Phyllis helps heavily pregnant mum Trudy Watts and her little boy Mickey escape from a violent husband – but the divorce laws make it hard for women in her position to break free. Trudy's suffering rekindles Sister Mary Cynthia's past trauma and her mental health deteriorates. Sister Ursula sends her away to the Mother House. There's joy for Patrick and Shelagh as she reveals she's pregnant – while Patsy is distraught to receive a letter from Hong Kong informing her of her father's terminal illness.

EPISODE TWO

The midwives struggle with Sister Ursula's iron-fist regime at Nonnatus House – particularly her demand that staff should not become emotionally involved with patients. When a new dad is burned by an explosion at a docklands warehouse, Shelagh and former army nurse Valerie Dyer help in the rescue, and Shelagh becomes involved with the subsequent legal fight for better work safety. The Turners share their happy news with the children, while Phyllis begins to understand the nature of Patsy and Delia's relationship. Patsy helps an expectant mother who faces a difficult birth due to achondroplasia, after which she resolves to help her sick father in Hong Kong, leaving Delia behind.

EPISODE THREE

Government changes to maternity care threaten the future of the maternity home and Dr Turner and Shelagh face a make-or-break inspection of their facilities. During the inspection, Shelagh is rushed to hospital with a threatened miscarriage. There's anger when Sister Ursula announces that the midwives must spend no longer than twenty minutes at each appointment and Trixie is appalled by the changes on her return from South Africa. Barbara's shortened visiting time means she fails to detect that Lucy Chen's baby has carbon monoxide poisoning due to a faulty heater and the child's life is almost lost. Chastened by events, Sister Ursula resigns her role and returns to the Mother House.

EPISODE FOUR

Debt-ridden single mum Marnie Wallace reluctantly agrees to give her forthcoming baby to her childless cousin but when the child arrives Marnie can't part with it. The case impacts on Tom, who was himself adopted. In hospital with her at-risk pregnancy, Shelagh befriends Gloria Venables, a woman in the same situation. The Turners are ultimately overjoyed to hear their infant's heartbeat but Gloria faces heartbreak. Sister Julienne's attempts to recruit a new midwife are unsuccessful, until she remembers army nurse Valerie Dyer, who happily accepts the job. Nurse Crane's Cubs win the community chariot race and Trixie gets herself and her Keep Fit ladies back into shape.

EPISODE FIVE

Fred's cousin Ivy Jackson dies suddenly, leaving Reggie, a twenty-one-year-old with Down's syndrome, alone in the world. Fred and Violet take him in but struggle with the practicalities and so seek a supportive residence for him. On a visit to an unsuitable mental health facility, Sister Mary Cynthia is discovered confined as an inpatient. Trixie helps a pregnant mother with bad dental health overcome her terror of the dentist and cures her own dislike of handsome dentist Christopher Dockerill. Phyllis gives Sister Winifred a driving lesson; Reggie finds his ideal home; the Turners make a house move and Nonnatus House welcomes new nurse Valerie Dyer.

EPISODE SIX

Poplar is anxious over the escalating Cuban Missile Crisis. Valerie cares for Nadifa Ghedi Jama, a pregnant first-time mother from Somalia – but the team are shocked to discover that she's undergone female genital mutilation, leading to a complicated birth and a clash of cultures. Sister Mary Cynthia is released from the mental institution and returns to Nonnatus House but her mental state worsens and a more gentle establishment is found for her permanent care. Trixie has a crisis of confidence about a second date with Christopher and a removals error means the Turners face the first night in their new home without furniture.

EPISODE SEVEN

Rhoda and Bernie Mullucks turn to Dr Turner for help to get their thalidomide-damaged daughter Susan fitted for artificial limbs. The experience causes renewed marital stress and pain for the parents, who reach out to others like themselves. Phyllis is devastated when she knocks down one of her Cub Scouts while driving her car, and faces potential legal consequences. Trixie suspects Christopher of another relationship but he reveals it's his child from a previous marriage. Moved by his disclosure, Trixie decides to share her own alcoholic secret with him.

EPISODE EIGHT

The midwives oversee the opening of a family planning clinic at the local community centre and mum-of-three Wilma Goddens is thrilled to get the new contraceptive pill. But tragedy strikes when Wilma dies of an embolism due to a side-effect. There's excitement when Barbara's wedding plans are brought forward so her father can officiate. And there's disappointment for Patrick when Shelagh excludes him from her impending birth plan. But when the labour finally comes, he's there to see the birth of baby Teddy. Tom's stag party brings a financial windfall that gives Barbara a priceless wedding present – the carousel ride she'd always treasured. And Delia's dreams are answered that night when Patsy returns from Hong Kong and seals their love with a kiss.

CHRISTMAS 1962

The infamous Big Freeze. Boxing Day brings deep snow and adverse weather, causing major disruption across Poplar. Trixie's holiday with Christopher is cancelled, while Valerie helps an unmarried couple living in a caravan to prepare for their new baby. The child is delivered premature and stillborn, and Valerie takes it sorrowfully back to Nonnatus House. But the baby unexpectedly revives and there is both joy and trauma for Valerie and the parents. Elsewhere, a local man's death leads Sister Julienne to discover a dark history of emotional and sexual abuse that kept a mother from her child. Tom gets a posting in Birmingham, while the weather forces Shelagh back to work at the surgery. Meanwhile, Phyllis is victorious over her new nemesis Sergeant Woolf when her Cubs succeed in bringing milk supplies to the snow-bound residents.

LIFE HAS ITS OWN PLANS

Stephen McGann

Dr Turner

For the Turners, Series Six marked a major watershed in the family's evolution: new life, as well as rites of passage for those family members already living. But their journey was a sharp reminder that evolution is neither smooth nor certain. It's a gift of chance and best endeavours, not a right. No family ever gets to decide how the future will pan out. That's why the way we travel matters and the reason the destinations we achieve feel so precious. I know this because, like the Turners, my own family's evolution has been a story of chance, medical care and best endeavours over expectations.

Series Six for the Turners began with the remarkable news that Shelagh, who'd been considered infertile after having TB, had fallen pregnant. Yet life had its own plans and Shelagh's miracle pregnancy was threatened by miscarriage. The crisis put a strain on Patrick's relationship with growing teenager Tim. Shelagh pulled through and Patrick conceded, over a shared beer, that his son wasn't a baby any more. Yet the life lessons kept coming. Even Shelagh's climactic labour with Teddy in episode eight was marked by a touching vulnerability, in spite of her being a professional midwife. The result was a beautiful new

addition to the family – but a family changed by experiences they had never expected or chosen.

And my own family? Well, Heidi and I had set out in our marriage years before, like Shelagh and Patrick, with expectations of a family at some future point of our choosing. We discovered that hidden medical issues had blighted chances of conception. Surgery was required to give Heidi any chance of a still-unlikely baby. So she underwent surgery and, miraculously, Dominic was conceived in a narrow window of fertility soon after. But a year later, serious complications arising from that surgery almost killed her, potentially leaving me, Patrick-like, as a grieving widower with a single baby son. Heidi survived, thanks to brilliant medical care, and we made it to now. One little family, eternally grateful to survive unchosen experience, and utterly changed by it.

That's why I think I felt every twist and turn of fate for the Turners in Series Six. I listened to that baby's heartbeat in episode four along with Patrick, desperate and relieved. And I waited outside the birthing-room door with him in episode eight – unable to help my wife in her moment of maximum distress. Because I'd been rough-schooled in the uncertainties that life can deal to even the most good-hearted of travellers.

The Turners are certainly good-hearted – although one or two viewers have told me they find their constant virtue a bit unsettling. 'Dr Turner is always so . . . nice!' they say – as if niceness in a dramatised human is rare enough to be a challenge to their suspension of disbelief! I disagree. I think the goodness in the Turner family is neither rare in real life nor detrimental to good TV drama. In fact, I think a key reason for the success of *Call the Midwife* is precisely that it doesn't subscribe to what you might call 'proper drama syndrome'.

There are certain clichés voiced about successful drama that are no less true for their overuse. 'Drama is about conflict' is one. Well, yes. All characters in an interesting story need someone or something conflicting with their progress in order to grow. Shelagh's conflicted birth progress in Series Six is a good example. Another well-worn cliché is that 'flawed characters are more interesting'. Which is true enough but insomuch as all characters are flawed – because all humans are flawed!

The interesting drama characters are simply those who expose their specific flaws to best dramatic effect. Dr Turner, for instance, is a war-damaged victim of PTSD, for whom certain situations induce short-temper, fragility, tension and crisis. A flawed human.

However, it's at this point that these common clichés can collide into an assumption about what supposedly makes 'proper' drama – meaning drama that is somehow more 'real' than other kinds. It's a common TV idea that a character's dark flaws are the only valid means of producing conflict. Every married couple in TV drama has therefore to manifest some terrible dark secret or betrayal, because . . . well, that's 'proper' drama, isn't it? The darker side of human nature. Murder drama, police drama, psychological thriller drama. That's clearly more real than, say, ordinary people having bad things happening to them but being basically nice to each other and trying to do their best.

But is it? Think about your friends. Your family. Your neighbours. Think of how many of them are serial killers, or bent coppers, or gun-toting gangsters. Yet check the TV schedules and note how many of those extreme characters and their dark flaws dominate the drama landscape. Do you know people like this yourself? Do their extremes define the way you live?

Now, think of how many people like the Turners you know. Decent people, to whom bad things can happen, yet who aren't innately bad themselves. Then tell me, what is the more 'proper' or 'real' drama? Is it the one that speaks to a common experience of ordinary goodness under challenge? Or one that lives only in the darkest fictional extremes of human nature? Both types of drama are perfectly valid – I enjoy watching both! – but I don't think the darkness of one makes it more 'real' or meaningful than the other. The opposite, in fact.

Bad things happen in *Call the Midwife*, as our viewers know. People die, get hurt, make mistakes and do bad things. Bad things happen to the Turners in Series Six. But darkness is something that besets them – they are not defined by it. And I believe that's true of wider society. *Call the Midwife* resonates intensely with our audience because it sings in harmony with most real lives and hopes.

Our drama understands that most humans strive for light, even when assaulted by darkness. We care about the best endeavours of the Turners because we share their desire to travel with hope, in spite of all flaws and conflicts. We are rooting for them to reach that precious destination they're aiming for because it's ours too – and their journey helps light our own way a little more clearly.

If ordinary goodness beset by life is not a 'proper' subject for drama, then perhaps drama has ceased to speak properly to us.

SOUTH AFRICAN SKIES

Jenny Agutter

Sister Julienne

Location shoots are always exciting and since I was a child what I've loved about the work I'm in has been going to different places. I can't tell you how much I love it; it's an adventure! South Africa was extraordinary and we felt rather like a theatre company on tour because at the end of a day's shooting we were all staying in the same place. Ten years on from the start of *Call the Midwife* we could all be hating each other by now but the absolute opposite is the case. There are no egos, nobody is trying to prove anything and we know when to give each other space.

It was wonderful to have Sinéad Cusack with us, playing the doctor in the Hope Clinic where the midwives went to help; we went off and did some things together – found restaurants to go to and a safari where they were taking special care of the animals. I felt a part of the group but I also love going off on my own so I went to Robben Island and for walks in Kirstenbosch, the big botanical gardens at the foot of Table Mountain. We were staying in Cape Town and we got to know the drivers and see different areas. The 300-year history of slavery, of abuse of people and of the land, apartheid and terrible poverty – that's so hard to be confronted with. You can't get past it and it yet exists alongside astounding vitality and a great spirit. As a visitor you're not involved; you see the beauty but oh, the despair.

The journey to work was a bit different to going to Longcross! It was an hour and a bit every morning, across great plains and fields, seeing ostriches, watching the sun rise. There was one memorable day when we filmed in one location and moved back to the other. Four of us were sitting in the back of a truck – Linda, Helen, Victoria and me – and when we were asked if we wanted to go in one of the official cars we all said, 'No, we want to stay in the truck!' So there we were, bouncing along these dirt-track roads, the sun coming down, dust in the air and we sang 'Amazing Grace'. It was like being in Australia when I was sixteen – the vast landscape is so much bigger than you.

Linda Bassett

Phyllis Crane

One trip back to base after a long day's filming was memorable. A few of us decided to travel in the back of the pick up truck that features in the episode. We sat on the floor with our backs to the cab and sang all the way 'home', watching the beautiful countryside unfold as we went by. My fellow actresses have stunning voices and can do harmonies – it was a real pleasure to sing with them.

Charlotte Ritchie

Barbara Gilbert

One of the best things about South Africa was being able to spend more time with the crew. You can often get a divide between the two worlds of cast and crew and I love to hang out with everybody. We really got to know each other well and that was a high point for me. We were there for a good month and there was time to talk, in the bar at the end of the day, on trips. It was a good storyline, bringing up the difficulties of missionary work and that whole idea of white saviours, swooping in to 'help' without thinking through the implications. Was it really the right thing to be doing? It was a tricky line to tread.

My lasting memory of the place is the light, the vast skies and the heat. The heat definitely got written into the script – there was a very funny moment when Phyllis sticks her nose in my armpit and says it's me that smells bad. There were lots of little moments like that between the characters and it makes it so real and human. Trixie's mascara running so she looks like a panda; Fred with a handkerchief on his head tied at each corner; everyone going pink rather than getting becomingly tanned; Barbara all sweaty with her fringe plastered to her forehead. When we went to the beach I had to wear this ruched swimming costume and the South African crew did a double take and said, 'You should get something on that sunburn,' and I was saying, 'It's FAKE!'

Then there was Tom proposing to Barbara and the grass engagement ring – that was very sweet and very Barbara to be fine with that.

Jack Ashton

Tom Hereward

I was in South Africa for three months altogether because, by complete coincidence, I'd got a job just before the *Call the Midwife* shoot in a docu-drama for National Geographic, filming just outside Cape Town (standing in for Iraq). We were all so excited to be there, especially Cliff Parisi, who really enjoyed, in his role as Fred Buckle, showing off his army-acquired expertise. Fred had been to El Alamein in North Africa with the British Expeditionary Force, digging long-drop toilets and picking up all sorts of useful knowledge. Cliff's a legend, and we became a very close-knit group, staying in the same place and having breakfast, tea, dinner, drinks together every day. And there was time off – I even went cage diving with sharks.

Cliff Parisi

Fred Buckle

I'd never been to South Africa before. The people were really lovely and welcoming, and it was just beautiful, but the contrast between the haves and have nots – that's a very bad juxtaposition. You could be driving through Cape Town seeing big houses with enormous gardens and a couple of miles down the road there are townships.

When I arrived, Jenny Agutter met me at the hotel reception and said she was going to take me on a route march to show me everything. She's the best, always has been, and my fourteen-year-old self was so excited but my older self had been travelling for eighteen hours non-stop and was desperate to go to sleep. I walked with her for about a mile and couldn't keep up; she's got so much energy. Then I said, 'I'm sorry but I've just got to go and get some sleep.' I lay there laughing, thinking if my fourteen-year-old self could see me now I'd slap myself!

The place we stayed in, we each had a cabin and they all looked the same. I went into Jenny's room once by accident, used the bathroom, laid myself down on the bed. What alerted me to the fact that it wasn't my room was that there was no TV. I thought, 'Funny, they must have come and taken it out,' and then I looked at the wall and thought – 'No filler holes. They can't have filled in the holes and painted over them in that time.' Even her suitcase was similar to mine.

Victoria Yeates

Sister Winifred

When we went to South Africa we nuns were beside ourselves with excitement. We got to have new clothes – white wimples! The day when four of us ended up riding back in an open truck at the end of the day's shooting, the sun setting, wild animals running about, was unforgettable. You pinch yourself and think, 'This is really special.' It was incredibly beautiful and we all got to spend a lot of time together – lots of laughing and talking and deep-and-meaningfuls. And I got engaged on that trip – my boyfriend came out to see me and proposed by a lake in an area that was populated by a lot of angry baboons.

Helen George

Trixie Franklin

The South Africa experience was wonderful because we all got to spend time together. In theatre, you go to the pub at the end of the show but in television you don't because you're so exhausted after long days. That was very special, being able to share and talk about our experiences of that incredible country. It's so beautiful and so messed up. There we were with security and drivers who live with the race issue and acute poverty. I felt very guilty for stepping into that. We still hear from one of

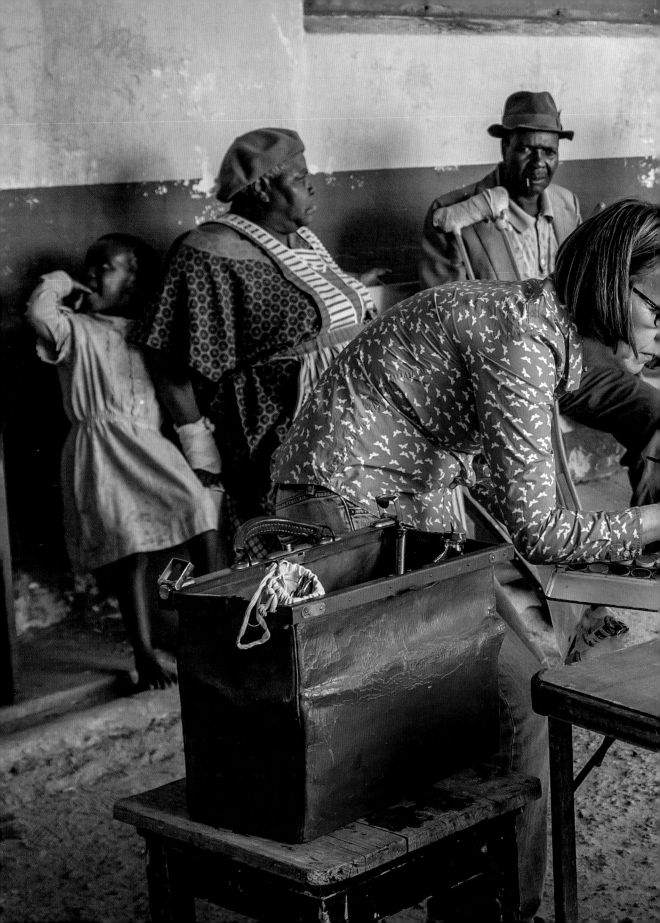

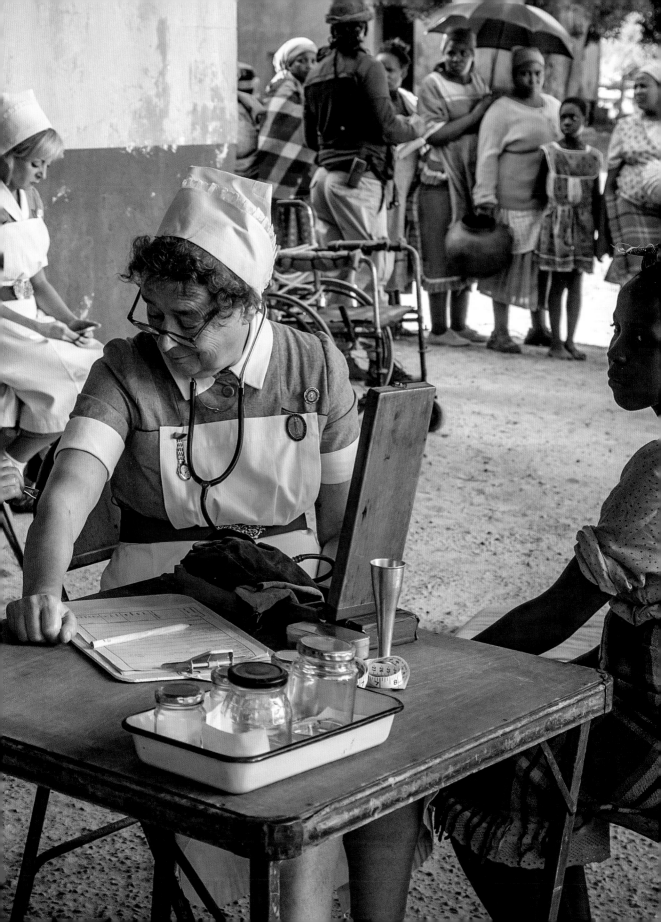

the drivers – the townships have been ravaged by Covid. His mother had died from it and he didn't have the money to bury her. There was no proper medical provision for her care and certainly no insurance. Life there is not just hard; it's cheap in a way that we can never understand.

Annie Tricklebank

Producer, Series 4–10

I've stayed in touch with some of the people we worked with in South Africa. They've been having a terrible time during the pandemic. We turned up there and we met people who were happy and delightful and generous though they had absolutely nothing. I hope we brought some good with us, that we at least let them know that there was somebody out there trying to tell their story, because it's not so different now to what it was then. Things have not moved on very much in terms of the way they live in townships. We were made to feel extremely welcome and safe and I'm very glad I went there.

Many of the stories on *Call the Midwife* affect you when you're making them. For all of its despair and tragedy, it's very warm – and it turns on a sixpence. You can go from crying to laughing within seconds. That's what happens in real life. Some of the events are heartbreaking and some make you angry, but what gives me joy and delight is that we might just be able to get something done somewhere along the way. A bit of happiness can be found.

SPECIAL FRIENDSHIP

Kate Lamb

Delia Busby

I have such respect and admiration for Linda Bassett. As Nurse Crane she was the only person who saw Delia and Patsy's relationship for what it was. And she could be tactful about it, without religion clouding her view. The scene I had with her when screenwriter Harriet Warner had written, 'The pain it costs to love – it is always worth it,' was so beautiful. I did zero acting in that scene because it just made me absolutely bawl. We had to go for a take where I was crying the least because she was so exquisite; in some I was crying from the moment she turned around. And that Lorca poem, that was the most beautiful moment:

> *For love of you, the air, it hurts,*
> *And my heart,*
> *And my hat, they hurt me.*

I read something similar to that only recently, about grief being love with nowhere to go.

GIVING BIRTH

Laura Main

Shelagh Turner

As Sister Bernadette, I think the first time I held a baby onscreen was in Series Two, in the episode about the twins, both played by Monica Dolan, one of whom had twins herself. I was in such awe of the actresses who 'gave birth' in front of the camera – it's a big deal and those days are really demanding – then in Series Six I had to do it myself!

Thank goodness we have Terri Coates; she's just amazing. Goodness knows how many births she's presided over. She recommended looking up natural childbirth on YouTube so I did, and then I had to just try not to worry about having to do the whole thing in front of colleagues. It was the first time the series had followed a pregnancy all the way through. Everybody was very supportive and shared their personal stories; they knew it was an exciting moment. It was my last day of filming that series and I just had to go for it. There was so much change to navigate for Sister Bernadette becoming Shelagh Turner, in a marriage, living with a man. It wasn't a happy ending straight away – it took a long time for her to blossom fully and feel comfortable in herself. The religious life wasn't for her in the end but her life became fuller and richer. She wanted a family but for a while that didn't happen and she lost the connection with her family of nuns, but that came back and she's now got a husband and four children, which wasn't quite what she'd anticipated.

BUCKLE UP

Cliff Parisi

Fred Buckle

Good old Fred, he's been there from the beginning. When I read the script for the first episode there wasn't much there for Fred and I thought, 'Not another one of these bloody jobs where you only get one line. I'm too long in the tooth for that – I'm not going to do it.' Luckily for me my wife had read the books and she said, 'No, you've got to do it, he's quite a central character.' Thank god she talked me into it.

I'm an East End boy myself, born in Hackney, and I like to think I'm quite handy but I'm not as much of a jack of all trades as Fred – I can fix stuff but it doesn't look pretty. He'd been working at Nonnatus House for quite some time before the nurses turned up, fixing the boiler, changing light bulbs, doing all the odd jobs. He's a lovely man – surrogate father to all the nurses, friendly manservant to the nuns. He seems to have a wise head on his shoulders. Life's taught him to take things slow and steady and not get too flustered. He's had his tragedies – when he came back from serving with the army in North Africa he found that his wife and daughters had been killed in the Blitz. The two eldest ones survived but he'd lost his family pretty much and I think the nuns may have looked after him then, helped him through that time. He started doing bits of work for them and ended up as a permanent fixture. In his funny way, he's a bit of a superhero, is Fred – puts on his overalls like a cape, fixes things, makes them good again, runs errands for Sister Julienne, rescues an abandoned baby from a dustbin, offers the odd word of advice to Sister Monica Joan and tells her off for grubbing around in his garden. He was always sorting out Sister Evangelina's bicycle and getting snapped at for not doing things properly. I loved working with Pam Ferris in that role. She was such a thunderous nun! The kind of woman I knew as a kid, who slaps you round the back of the head, then shoves a sixpence in your hand and tells you to run off and buy yourself some sweets. Shooting the scene when she dies overnight, sitting in her armchair by the fire, and Fred finds her – that was incredibly moving and not easy to do.

The episode with Fred getting a pig was quite something. The costume department wanted to make it look as if I was covered in mud so they smeared Nutella everywhere. I was supposed to run after this pig but all it wanted to do was to stay close to me and lick the Nutella off my boots. Heidi manages to keep producing these brilliant, top-quality scripts – and they turn from laughter to tragedy and right back again.

For quite a while, Fred was dealing exclusively with nuns, nurses, children, Cub Scouts – no love interest for him. He was allowed someone to play cards with occasionally or to go for a booze-up in the pub with but he was in a world where he was the only man apart from Dr Turner. That was his comfort zone in a way, until he met Violet. She's brilliant, Annabelle Apsion – posh totty with a great sense of humour. And now there's Daniel Laurie as Reggie as well – I love that young man and he's a really good actor, fabulous to work with. When you think about it, Fred started out pretty much as just a guy who walked through a shot with a toolbox, muttered something helpful, delivered a bit of plot and now he has a family. It adds a completely different dimension – Violet's acceptance of Reggie showing how deep her love is for Fred; Reggie calling her Mum; Violet buying a frame for the photograph of Fred's dead wife and wrapping it up; Fred and Violet's tenderness with each other, their business ventures.

Annabelle Apsion

Violet Buckle

The quality of acting on the show is superb – that's always very exciting. Before I joined, I was so jealous that I hadn't been cast in the original series that I couldn't bear to watch it! I was asked to audition for a guest role with an extremely sad and upsetting storyline, and I thought to myself, 'If I accept this, I'll never be able to be a regular'. Then, out of the blue, I was invited to join the cast and that was really lovely. I'd much rather be in as a regular member and I really like the character. She's interesting and she keeps developing.

I've always been drawn to questions about the meaning of life and how we treat each other. I love the extra dimension we have in *Call the Midwife* – social history and the thread that runs through it of treating everyone as equally important within the community. Also, the good that shines from people who are motivated to serve – the midwives, Dr Turner, the nuns. Like many people, I've had some unpleasant experiences with religious figures so it's lovely to see people who want to serve Christ and to serve others – who aren't hypocrites or abusers or sadists. The church has attracted people who have used their power to hurt rather than to help and on *Call the Midwife* most of the characters are fundamentally good. Awful things happen – death and illness and violence and deprivation – but ultimately goodness comes through. Unfortunately, there's an obsession in media stories these days with stirring up fear and suspicion, making us frightened of other people. It's completely the opposite on *Call the Midwife* and I think that really is an antidote.

When I was in New Zealand a while ago, I was walking on the Milford Track and someone I passed said, 'Oh, it's you!' It was this young American woman and she told me that she and her colleague worked for an anti-slavery charity and travelled around parts of Africa and India where there is still illegal slavery. They used to download episodes of *Call the Midwife* and watch one every night. She said it was very cathartic because they had to hold everything together during the day – you can imagine what awful things they were encountering. The show is weepy, it does make people cry, but it's not so much distress as the connection to fundamental goodness. In spite of loss, of fear, there's something that pulls us through. I thought it was astonishing that two young women could do such intrepid, frightening work and then watch our show for solace. What an honour to be in something that has such potency, that makes people feel sustained, calmed, comforted and inspired.

Violet's menopause story was marvellous – and definitely made a connection. It was refreshing and funny and true and people could really relate to that. It was quite hard for make-up, though, having to show my hot flushes!

The onscreen relationship between the Buckles – Violet, Fred and Reggie – is lovely. We do genuinely enjoy all our scenes together. I think one of the nicest perks about being an actor is that you get to meet the most gorgeous people. We have a terrific time and love being with one another. The great motivating quality of kindness is very evident on this show – everyone is so nice, and talented. And we're doing something that feels of value.

It's difficult to pinpoint a favourite moment for Violet but I did love it when Reggie first came. Violet had been a bit off with him. She's sewing the hem of his trousers and he says something about feeling bad that he's happy when his mother has just died and she says, 'Your mum would want you to be happy.' It changed how she saw Reggie. She saw him for who he was and how loving he was. Daniel did that scene so beautifully; he's incredibly sensitive. I also like Violet's activities as a councillor. I'm interested in politics so I'm living vicariously through her, looking to solve problems around housing and social welfare. When it comes to the practicalities of helping people she's very down to earth and non-partisan, she doesn't have attitude.

Daniel Laurie

Reggie Jackson

It's so funny that Annabelle said that Violet wasn't sure about Reggie to begin with because I was thinking about that. Now they're a really good family together – Fred and Violet didn't have children and they brought Reggie into their life. I love working with Cliff and Annabelle – they're awesome. Reggie has a particular look and I like that; it's a part of who he is. The make-up people have this gel for the hair and they make it really smooth. He has round glasses and those cardigans he wears are brilliant, really well made. And the hat that Nurse Crane hand-knitted for him for Christmas.

There are so many good things but I think I do have a favourite moment. It goes like this. I started out on *Call the Midwife* in Series Six, episode five, and I related to Reggie as a character because I've been bullied in my past so playing him is a way to explore and discover what he's like. He's courageous. There is so much about him that is true personally for me too. It was difficult to play that first episode. We all cried but it was really good.

It is a challenge to learn the lines but I like preparing and getting it right. Then sometimes you have to do other things as well, like learning ballroom dancing. You have rehearsals for that but then you're on set and you just get on with it, remembering those steps and all the moves.

EXPLOSIVE ENTRY

Jennifer Kirby

Valerie Dyer

My first episode was quite something – rushing off to try to help when there's an explosion at one of the dockyard warehouses. It was a bit different to join as one of the midwives who actually comes from the East End and who has first-hand experience of living and working there. That really spoke to me. I'd been a fan of the show from the beginning – it started when I was at drama school, at LAMDA. After long, sloggy weeks and twelve-hour days it was a Sunday-night treat. On Mondays, we'd talk about what television we'd watched at the weekend and people would say, 'Jen, you should be in that show, it suits you.'

When I got the part I was incredibly excited but it felt too good to be true. In the acting business you always assume you're not going to get something. When you do it feels like – really? You don't quite trust it.

Then the first episode turned out to be a bit tricky in a completely unexpected way. I did the audition on tape because I was in New York, in a show with the RSC. I managed to break my foot, running offstage, so I had to wear one of those boots. It was due to come off just in time for *Call the Midwife* but when I got the script the first thing I had to do was run and it also said that you'd hear Valerie's heels clacking down a hallway. I thought, 'Argh! Heels, an explosion, running, how will I manage?'

ROUNDABOUT WEDDING

Charlotte Ritchie

Barbara Gilbert

Barbara was so practical – she just wanted to wear comfortable clothes and have this sensible, short haircut. For my first series it was like a shiny conker – I had a completely round head. I'd get my hair back-brushed really big and then made into that style. I can't believe women did that every day. But of all the periods in fashion not to be glamorous! I was always very jealous of Trixie's outfits and Patsy's slacks. For Barbara, it was a huge treat if I got to wear a bit of eyeliner. I remember begging for it.

The wedding was lovely and there was a lot of excitement around it, with all the preparations, having Phyllis as my bridesmaid. The dress was amazing and that wonderful cape – this modest girl going out on a limb for once. It made me realise how unsentimental I am because it wasn't until I actually put on the dress that I could see how it was quite cool.

It was a late shoot and such fun to film. The carousel was glorious. There was lots of footage of the nuns going round and round but I think most of that didn't make the cut. It was an absolutely joyful thing.

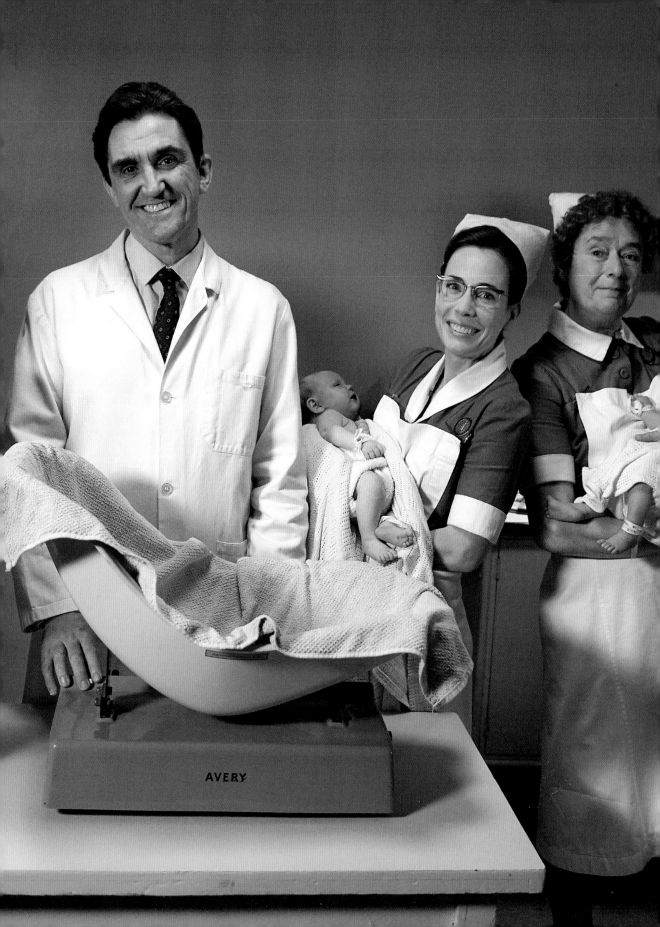

SERIES SEVEN

1963

EPISODE ONE

The Big Freeze continues and, with Barbara gone, Sister Julienne recruits a new midwife. Nurse Lucille Anderson arrives in heavy snow, sick and days late. She earns respect when dragged from her sick bed to help with a breech birth. An exotic dancer wants to give up her baby for adoption but bonds with her after a rhesus blood problem creates complications. Phyllis and Dr Turner care for Ruth Gelin, an elderly Jewish woman suffering from bowel cancer. The Gelins face eviction as the street is demolished but Phyllis forces Sergeant Woolf to delay work until Ruth has died. Trixie takes her relationship with Christopher to the next level and Sister Winifred has driving-test nerves.

EPISODE TWO

West Indian Lucille faces bigotry when hairdresser Marjory Chivvers suffers a stroke after birth and her mother, Mae Stanton, singles Lucille out for blame. The team rally to protect their newest recruit and restore Lucille's confidence in their community. Sister Winifred wants fathers to be more involved in the birth but football coach Allan Romaine isn't so sure. However, he ends up involved in his own child's impromptu birth in the back of his minibus. The arrival of beautiful Hungarian au pair Magda shakes up the Turner household; Trixie's night in with Christopher is a culinary disaster, while Phyllis and Sergeant Woolf lock horns when he finds her car abandoned for an emergency birth.

EPISODE THREE

Trixie and Phyllis are involved in the tragic case of Doreen Lunt, diagnosed with the degenerative disorder Huntington's disease. Doreen quickly deteriorates to the point where she's unable to look after her children but the inherited nature of Huntington's has consequences for the whole family. Fred and Violet organise a beauty contest, while concern for Christopher's divorce-torn daughter leads Trixie to end their relationship and she turns back to drink. Au pair Magda discovers she's pregnant and steals ergometrine from Nonnatus House in an attempt to terminate the pregnancy, putting her life in danger and losing her job.

EPISODE FOUR

Pakistani wife Mumtaz Gani, who has accepted her own childlessness, is heartbroken when her husband brings home a second wife who is eight months pregnant. Sister Julienne must help Mumtaz find a way to accommodate these family changes for all their sakes. Lucille cares for a pregnant mother with an unusual craving for coal; Fred persuades Sister Monica Joan to consent to much-needed cataract surgery, while Phyllis confronts Trixie about her return to drink. Trixie avoids the issue but eventually accepts her need to confront it. She takes a six-month break from Nonnatus House.

EPISODE FIVE

There's fear and panic in Poplar when a rumour spreads that a newly arrived Nigerian sailor has smallpox and the race is on to find where he's hiding. Dr Turner discovers that he is suffering from leprosy and the team are able to find a place for him to be treated. Lucille needs all of her relaxation skills to help a mother with a phobia of giving birth, following a previous traumatic delivery. Reggie arrives home in time to help Fred and Violet organise the parish picnic, while Tom and Barbara return to find a picnic-deserted Nonnatus House.

EPISODE SIX

An Irish family arrives in Poplar to run the local newsagents but husband Terry Davidson is tragically killed in a car crash. Pregnant widow Pearl struggles to cope and when the shop is damaged by fire, Fred and the team help Pearl and the family get back on their feet. Valerie and Lucille give sex education classes for teens but a stern mother complains. The mother's attitude is rooted in her sister's promiscuous behaviour and Valerie helps her track down her missing sibling who'd been cruelly committed to an asylum. Sister Monica Joan goes to hospital for cataract surgery but finds her peace shattered by talkative fellow patient Maudie Valentine. Barbara is rushed to hospital when her flu is suspected to in fact be septicaemia.

EPISODE SEVEN

A stricken Tom waits in the hospital for news of Barbara as her condition worsens. Her absence means that Nonnatus House must pull together, with even Shelagh returning to midwifery duties. Dr Turner assists at a remand home, where young inmate Michael Sumpter is depressed and bullied. The Turners resolve to help in Michael's court case, so that he might be reunited with his new child. Lucille cares for Jamaican pastor's wife Alecia Palmer and is invited to join their home church congregation. Nonnatus House is rocked to its core when Barbara's meningococcal sepsis worsens and she dies. The team unite in shock and grief.

EPISODE EIGHT

After Barbara's moving funeral, the team are right back to work with an unexpected influx of mothers after a nearby maternity home closes. Grief-stricken Phyllis returns to work but is incapacitated with a bad back. She's impatient with a young woman but softens when the teenager's fear becomes clear and the birth of her baby ultimately brings Phyllis comfort. Lucille tends to pregnant Olive Mawson who's moved back in with her widowed father after her failed marriage. When he reveals his long-term relationship with a man who now has dementia, Olive must find a way to share her future with both of them. The team pull through and Sister Monica Joan is distracted from President Kennedy's televised funeral to attend her surprise birthday party involving the whole community.

CHRISTMAS 1963

The Order's Mother Superior is dying and the nuns must return to the Mother House to vote for her successor. Sister Julienne is the obvious replacement and her future at Nonnatus House therefore hangs in the balance. Indefatigable Sister Mildred arrives with a group of orphaned children from Hong Kong for adoption and forthright Miss Higgins arrives as the new surgery receptionist. When a mother is stranded in labour, Trixie, Valerie and Lucille deliver the baby in the street. The team head to the Mother House where Sister Winifred is moved by the unclaimed orphans there. They encounter pregnant Lena Tremblay, a former orphan and Australian child migrant, whose life is still haunted by the forced separation from her little brother. The team set about finding Lena's brother and reuniting them. And when one of the orphans, May, fails to find a new home, the Turners decide to take her themselves.

CALL THE MIDWIFE 7
ROLL A563 SLATE 3258 TAKE 5
SCENE 7/11
DIR: SYDNEY MACARTNEY
DOP: STUART BIDDLECOMBE
DATE: 27TH OCT '17

THE BIG FREEZE

Stephen McGann

Dr Turner

Series Seven provided us with an historical event – one that would certainly have impacted on the midwives working in early 1963. It was known as the 'Big Freeze', a period of brutal arctic weather that affected the whole of Great Britain, blocking roads with snow drifts and cutting off whole communities. These conditions commenced in December and didn't let up until April. The series also passed a much smaller historical milestone, which subtly changed my relationship with the period drama I was part of. I was born in the February of that Big Freeze. *Call the Midwife* had therefore gone from being a period drama I worked on to a part of my own living history!

Believe it or not, I was also delivered at home, Nonnatus style, by a midwife who arrived on a bicycle through a blizzard. My dad sat on the stairs in the hall, shut out of the bedroom and listening to my mum's labour. You can practically hear the *Call the Midwife* theme music. Well . . . maybe not. The midwife was apparently in a foul mood for being called out unexpectedly at night in such awful weather! Not exactly a Nonnatun temperament. As I'm fond of saying, I was born apologising for any inconvenience caused.

Filming our Big Freeze involved building up large pretend snow mounds on the street and then covering everything with a specialist

'fake snow' material that looks absolutely authentic but smells strangely of burnt paper!

It was a strange feeling to think that *Call the Midwife* had now entered the timespan of my own life, and that I'd joined those senior members of the cast who were alive when the events we portray took place. And significant, too. *Call the Midwife* is a period drama that takes place in very recent history – it's not a remote Edwardian or Victorian world. For many people, it's their own past, or the past of an older relative. The medical and social changes taking place in the early 1960s London of Series Seven are still evident in the world today. Many of those social changes are still unfolding – like women's rights or medical advancements. Others may feel more uncertain, or less optimistic than they were – such as in regards to the functioning of our national health system or the clashes of our cultures. But those changes are close enough in *Call the Midwife* to see how we got from there to here and the good reasons why our society might have set out to do those things in the first place.

One social change evident in Series Seven is present in the person of new nurse Lucille Anderson, played by Leonie Elliott. Lucille arrived as part of a wave of Caribbean nurses recruited by the National Health Service to help the health system cope with the expansion taking place. That in turn was part of a bigger wave of immigration from former colonies of the United Kingdom to feed the new post-war economic boom. The East End, like Britain, was changing – new housing, new jobs, unfamiliar races and cultures. *Call the Midwife* has followed this process of social change carefully over time, in keeping with the slow progress of the years. As the sixties progressed, these communities played an ever-greater part of the work the midwives did.

For Leonie, it was an enormous responsibility – not only to arrive as a new lead character on a hit show but also to represent in microcosm a watershed moment of cultural change. She handled it in typical Leonie style: thoughtfully, intelligently and with a constant attention to detail. Leonie is a north Londoner from a family of West Indian heritage. She is sharp, well educated and quietly courageous in her approach to her work. She immediately sought out members of her extended family for research on dialect and cultural practices at that time – which was a huge bonus for our production. Stories and experiences from her family were used as research material for Series Seven and beyond. An example of this was the nature of the 'house churches' that churchgoing Caribbean communities formed as an alternative to the traditional British churches, where many of the new arrivals didn't feel welcome. Lucille's new church provided an immensely moving *Call the Midwife* moment in episode seven – the singing of 'Amazing Grace' by the congregation following Barbara's death.

A lot of grace was required by Lucille in episode two when she faced discrimination in her work and was unfairly blamed for a mother's stroke. *Call the Midwife* has never been scared to show the darker side of social change evident in those years as it's a programme that has the value of all humans at its heart. To walk in that light one also has to acknowledge the shadows. Leonie brought an immense dignity and character to those themes and gave our drama a fresh moral impetus. Also, she became one of my favourite people to make laugh on set! When she gets the giggles it's truly infectious – and she has a fine sense of the absurd. Which is fortunate, as my humour does tend towards the childish . . .

Series Seven was certainly not all laughs. There was the devastating death of Barbara, with the departure of the adored Charlotte Ritchie. I still miss the wonderful Ms Ritchie – yet there's something resolutely lifelike about *Call the Midwife's* ability to say goodbye to its own and bring in new blood. Nonnatus House is both a religious and a nursing community; both of these types of community are transient by nature. Over the years, they can see many changes of personnel. The character changes we've seen in ten years of *Call the Midwife* reflects the reality of those who go wherever care is needed. And, of course, death has its own way of bringing change. Sister Evangelina. Barbara. Death is a part of life: a loss that can't be avoided but which adds meaning to the life of those who remain.

So Series Seven was the year when *Call the Midwife* became living history for me. A time of cold and comfort; of new friends made and old ones lost; of frozen attitudes and warmer cultures; of the past demolished and fresh futures built in their place; of hymns sung and tears shed.

And all of that with the faint aroma of burnt paper!

SNOWY START

Leonie Elliott

Lucille Anderson

It was quite a strange start for me because it was the Big Freeze, with fake snow blowing all over the place, and Lucille had to make a dramatic entrance, tripping up on the doorstep of Nonnatus House and then getting ill almost immediately and having to stay in bed. I was all ready to get going and then I had to stop. It was something to play against though, an immediate tension and duality, which is interesting. She's a great character – self-assured and driven but with a kind of poise and restraint as well. It's partly her religious belief, I think, and partly the way she was brought up in Jamaica.

These days we're all encouraged to share how we feel in terms of both our mental health and our physical health. I always get the feeling from my grandparents that it was very different for them – they believed that the most important thing was to have a strong belief and to hold yourself together. There was a pride in that resilience. I started asking them about their experiences and I hadn't heard any of these stories so I got to know so much more about their lives in their twenties, when they first arrived from Jamaica. It wasn't straightforward to join a church; you could attend a service and you'd be asked politely to leave afterwards. I asked my grandad what would happen if you were religious and wanted to join a church but were not allowed in. He said, 'We'd set up

our own' – so that's how the services in living rooms began. It must have been such a culture shock to them, settling in London and trying to find like-minded souls. My grandparents have all this knowledge to pass on and when they got talking they had gems to share. Heidi Thomas is amazing – so inquisitive and always wanting to learn and understand, and that's how my grandparents' story ended up being incorporated in the show.

The issue of racism is something that we had to tackle because of the period – it's a sad part of Lucille's story and that of anyone from the Windrush generation. We'd be doing those stories and experiences a disservice if we didn't touch on it and the sorry truth is that it would be romanticising the London of the time if we failed to address that. Londoners were fairly hostile then, and ignorant, but I always say that it's a part of Lucille's story but not the whole of it. That's so important.

I thought I was quite used to babies until I started work on *Call the Midwife!* It's pretty daunting, and it's not just holding them; it's working with an actress and a baby and making it look as if you're famil- iar with the business of giving birth. At my first birth I remember thinking, 'Oh my goodness me, there's a lot going on here!' And now, in my fourth series, it really has, oddly, become second nature. I feel a lot more relaxed and the babies respond to that – in my first series there were a lot of crying babies! Terri Coates is brilliant at giving exactly the right advice at the right moment. When you weigh a baby you wrap it up in this sling with a hook on and you have to pick it up and let it hang – it has to look like second nature and it's not. Terri makes it look so easy, then you try and it looks completely the opposite. In between takes there's a lot of practising.

A REAL PREGNANCY

Helen George

Trixie Franklin

It was pretty remarkable to embark on my relationship with Jack through the show and to end up pregnant while we were both working on it – and by then, his character, Tom Hereward, was in love with Barbara and had married her. Just a bit complicated! It wasn't right in the storyline for Trixie to get pregnant so I had to cover it up for as long as I could. I was very gung-ho about it and didn't want the lines to be blurred but it did become more and more of a challenge. Paddy Blake, the cameraman, and I had to make it work somehow, and the costume department provided imaginative solutions, like a cape and a very bulky fake-fur coat. There was a lot of sitting down whenever I could and hiding half of me behind other people – as Heidi said, 'It's amazing what you can conceal with the help of a swing coat and a clipboard.' I must admit that I thought my experience on *Call the Midwife* might be of some help but it really wasn't. I knew how to hold a baby but that didn't prepare me for what a struggle the feeding turned out to be, for example. We didn't do NCT (National Childbirth Trust) antenatal classes, and I think we probably should have.

BABIES CALL
THE SHOTS

Syd Macartney

Director on Series 5–10

Fortunately, I love babies – I find them fascinating – but it's nice to give them back at the end of the day! When a baby's on set it controls the way things are going to go. The actors have to fall in line and if the baby's not happy, not in the right emotional state, we have to wait until it is. They have an absolute hold over you.

Terri Coates is a real force – she has a way of swinging the babies when they're crying to get them to settle and it usually works like a charm, but not always. Sometimes there's a crew of around forty of us standing around thinking, 'Please, baby, be quiet!' It's mad, really, all of us waiting for this little creature who basically either wants to be fed or to go to sleep. Terri's a great one for pulling us up if things don't look realistic but she understands the dramatic perspective as well. Now when I see a birth on a different programme I'm tut-tutting and thinking, 'That's totally unbelievable! That's not a labour pain!' I've become a birth bore. My daughter is currently pregnant with twins and I'm always offering her unwanted advice. I lean back in my chair and make remarks, like, 'The second one's probably going to be breach; you do know that, don't you?' 'Yes, thanks, Dad.' Raised eyebrows.

KEEPING AN EYE
ON THE DETAIL

Julia Castle

Production designer, Series 8–10

I've been with the show from the beginning and when I started the art department consisted of only five people. My job was props buying and research, making sure that babies' bottles were the right shape, that sort of thing. Now I've moved up to be production designer. The research is very detailed and I love doing it. My book collection is huge, particularly photography books. There's a lot to draw on from photographs of streets and not necessarily just in London – there are amazing pictures of the Glasgow slums. You get the feel of a place, the standard of living, and sometimes I might see a picture of a person that fits with the script and gives me a focus to build my design on. There was a wonderful picture of an old man in braces and baggy trousers looking after his pigeons that did exactly that. I also use a lot of vintage DIY magazines for colours. They give you a more real colour palette – if you look at a magazine like *Homes & Gardens*, that would be posher. DIY publications give you a very good idea of what young, aspirational people would have been doing. They couldn't afford to have it done; they'd have been saving up and doing it for themselves.

Then there are catalogues from the right years, so you can see what prams would have looked like then, or kitchen appliances. It is a drama, not a documentary, but we want it to look right, to get the essence of it. And there's always someone who'll let you know if you get something wrong! There was a woman who was insistent that we'd got the lining of a pram wrong so that's why I like photographs and knowing when they were taken and magazines – if I see a headboard in a 1965 magazine then I know for sure it existed at that time.

We use modern things sometimes and adapt them or paint them. Hiring gets very expensive over time so it can be better to make and own things, like the hospital beds. We had those made, and the telephone box. The nice thing about owning is that we can distress things, break them down. If you go to auctions or house clearances you can often buy what you want for the same price as hiring. We don't go to hire companies much because we want our things to look individual and specific. I catch myself watching another show on television sometimes and thinking, 'That sofa's from *All Creatures Great and Small.*' Specialist medical items we hire but if it's domestic we always try and buy. Nobody's house is perfectly co-ordinated with matching sets of everything.

I have what's known as 'the bible' in my office with all the pieces of furniture in it so I can flick through and spot a chair that could be reupholstered if the colour or pattern isn't right. It's a process of making things look different but using the same things over and over again. And we're very ingenious – the tunnel that they walk through to get to Nonnatus House, we reverse that and if you shoot from the other direction we make it a garage, with a market street on the other side.

Now that the Buckles have got a newsagents we have to stock it and we're often not allowed to use branded products for legal reasons so we make a lot of stuff ourselves. Packs of cigarettes, sweets – I've had a whole team of people making those; they get a whole table-load done, you put it on set and it's swallowed up. You realise you need ten times as much.

My brilliant set decorator, Dean Lee, has a fantastic eye for detail. It's ideal to have someone who has the opposite skills to you. I'm very much a big-picture person and he's small, minute picture. He checks flower arranging from 1960s books and looks through cookery books for ideas about food, how they'd have done their potato salad, halved hard-boiled eggs with a whirly bit of salad cream on top, curly parsley for garnish.

Charlotte Ritchie

Barbara Hereward

I never got over how little time the crew have to create what you see on screen – the turnaround time is so quick. Once, we were filming outside in the docks, and between one scene and the next they turned the space into something that looked like a painting – a bar with smoke and half-finished pints – and my jaw just dropped. I remember saying, 'How have you done that?' As actors we get to be the face of the show but we go in and out while the crew transform spaces within a day. *Call the Midwife* looks the way it does because of the work behind the camera by the art department, lighting, all those people – it's epic.

A NATION
MOURNS

Charlotte Ritchie

Barbara Hereward

The show makes me cry anyway, every single episode without fail, but Barbara's death was almost too sad. People got quite angry with me for dying. And it is very hard to act a death when you know that people are going through those tragedies for real – part of you thinks that it's really wrong to be acting it out, lying on a bed and imagining that you're not going to live for much longer. Doing that while knowing that I was also leaving the programme was very emotional, especially when I had two such important people on either side of me – Linda and Jack as Phyllis and Tom. They were so beautiful in those scenes, showing their grief and their need to be strong and keep going. I'm getting a prickly nose just thinking about it.

Part of me hoped that Barbara wouldn't have to leave in such a final, irreversible way but it was quite cathartic to go and for the door to be properly closed behind me. I have such an attachment to that character – her journey was beautifully told, this complete scatterbrain becoming stoic and solid by the end. She became a big chunk of who I was, who I am.

Linda Bassett

Phyllis Crane

Barbara's death came as a shock to us and we felt it. Charlotte and Jack were both wonderful and great colleagues. Charlotte and I started in the same year, in Series Four, and after a rocky start our characters became close friends – Phyllis was surprised and touched to be asked to be Barbara's bridesmaid. She was with her when she died, sharing Psalm 23 with Tom when he couldn't go on. Phyllis is a rare atheist in Nonnatus House, but she grew up with Psalms and Hymns and takes pleasure in their beauty.

Jack Ashton

Tom Hereward

Filming that was memorable in a lot of ways. Helen and I thought we'd planned it all perfectly – she finished shooting when she was eight months pregnant but our daughter Wren came early. I had a call asking me if I could very kindly come in and do the scenes, so I did, not having slept since Wren was born the day before. I was an emotional wreck in every way, thinking about Helen and Wren, and saying goodbye both to Barbara and to someone I'd been working with for four years. It was all a bit of a blur but I think it came out all right and it was very honest and very raw as always. One minute Barbara was all right and the next she was gone. Another instance of *Call the Midwife* raising awareness of a condition that can easily get overlooked – it was blood poisoning, septicaemia, and that can move very fast.

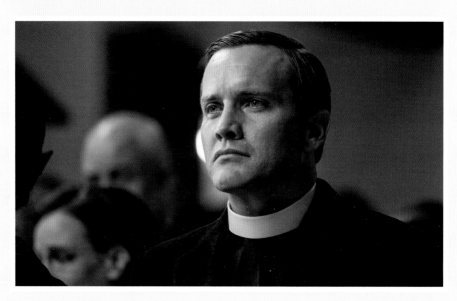

Syd Macartney

Director on Series 5–10

Sometimes when you work with actors real emotion can threaten to take over – you need control because you're having to tell the story in a certain way and if it's too real it sometimes sidesteps what you're trying to do. As a director, I married Barbara and then I watched her die. There've been a few times in my career, and this was one of them, when I found myself watching the performance and I couldn't help myself, I was touched by it. But unfortunately that means that you lose objectivity and you have to guard against that. When you look at it cold in the cutting room a few weeks later you have to make sure that it's truthful on the screen and not just living in your heart. That's where the film-making process gets really interesting for me, when you take what you did on the day and by editing it together and modifying it a little, you – hopefully – make it better.

MAKING THE MUSICAL CONNECTION

Maurizio Malagnini

Composer, Series 4–10

My music is Italian, like me, in that I think I have inherited some of the musical characteristics from composers such as Bellini, who wrote glorious long melodies – if he was alive now he could write wonderful film scores. Then there's Rossini and his incredible skill with crescendos – I need those for the birth scenes. And Puccini, who is so good at defining the environment around a character – for example, the writing for the clarinet in *La Bohème*, which conjures up the feeling of cold. It's hard to do that with words but with music you can use cold harmonics, you can make the audience feel that the room is cold. I've learnt so much from later composers, too, who wrote famous film scores, like Nino Rota and Ennio Morricone. From Rota how melody can define a character, like Burt Lancaster in *The Leopard*, and from Morricone how you can find a musical element that works in many different scenes. Every time the music is played it acquires more power, a little bit like an avalanche that starts small and then gathers weight and force. There are themes in the music I've written for *Call the Midwife* that represent the creation of life, the strength of life, and they repeat and grow with every variation. There is no accent in music – it's international, universal – you just hear the human emotion.

The way it works is that I get sent an entire episode and I watch it with the director and the producer, Annie Tricklebank, and we decide where the music should go. It's a decision that sometimes is very clear and sometimes not so much so we discuss and decide between us. Then I go home to my studio and I play the piano as I compose and bring in all the different instruments on the computer. The piano stays as my performance and the rest gets put into a score by an orchestrator. For many, many episodes I have worked with Jean Stephan, who used to take the Eurostar from Paris for every episode but this year we have been working remotely. Then we go to record, with the finest British players from different orchestras – the Royal Philharmonic, the London Symphony Orchestra, the Chamber Orchestra of London, the Royal Ballet orchestra – and after that there is dubbing, which is the process of mixing the music and film and sound effects. We watch the episode again and this time with Pippa Harris and Heidi. From the corner of my eye I can see her and after a while she will start crying, which is a very good sign for me. She says, 'You made me cry,' and I say, 'No, *you* made *me* cry.' That means to me that it has done what music should do; it's made a connection. I can speak best with music, not words, and it's a great privilege on *Call the Midwife* to help that connection, to make a bridge between the story and the audience.

CHRISTMAS SURPRISE

Miriam Margolyes

Sister Mildred

My first appearance was in the Christmas special for 1963 and as far as I was concerned, it really was like all my Christmases coming at once. I was shameless about wanting to be in the show – I dropped a hint every time I was on television. Eventually I was on *This Morning* and I made an absolutely direct appeal without any sort of flannel: 'Look, if you're watching, I want to be in *Call the Midwife*, please, I don't mind what I play.' Mind you, I was imagining that they'd use me as a Jewish East End housewife, not as an Anglican nun – that never crossed my mind! I think it is in every sense a good programme. The production values are high, the moral values are high, the acting and writing are of the very highest quality and it's truthful – it's about real people in real situations. When I was asked to join it was a very glorious moment. Everybody welcomed me into the gang and I feel extraordinarily lucky to be a part of it.

My experience of midwifery is not exclusively through my portrayal of Dickens's Mrs Gamp – she is not an example to follow. I certainly didn't base Sister (now Mother) Mildred on her, they are worlds apart. But I have played an Egyptian gynaecologist, in the late 1970s, in a film called *The Awakening* directed by Mike Newell. Charlton Heston and Susanna York were in it, and Jill Townsend, with her legs in stirrups, and me having to deliver her baby. I was supposed to use forceps and I kept dropping them on the floor. I'm not good with my hands; it was a bit of a disaster.

I love the values of the programme – compassion and honesty and showing people being vulnerable. It's very heartening because most of the stuff we see on television is cruel. I can enjoy that as well but it's important that there is a programme like *Call the Midwife*, which I do not consider to be sentimental. It's about feeling; not over-feeling but genuine emotion. People working with a determination to show compassion and give practical help, never to make judgements. That's set up by Vanessa Redgrave doing the narration at the beginning and the end. She's the queen of voiceover. I may be more versatile – after all, she doesn't do sex tapes – but she's the top. It was funny because I did an 'in conversation' article with her for the *Guardian* recently and she didn't know that I was playing Mother Mildred. I was quite miffed.

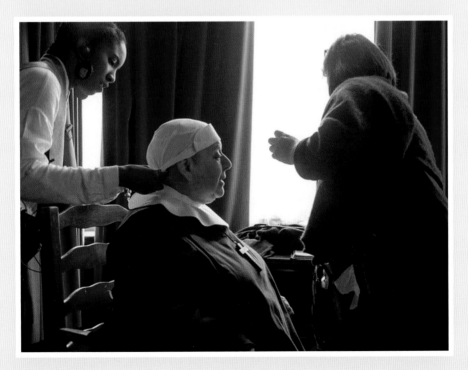

SERIES EIGHT

1964

EPISODE ONE

Spring arrives and Nonnatus House welcomes two new nuns from the Mother House: worldly-wise Sister Hilda and newly qualified Sister Frances. Lucille cares for expectant mother Leslie whose sister Cath, an aspiring model, develops a dose of food poisoning. When this is revealed to be in fact a botched back-street abortion, Valerie and Sister Frances must help Cath deal with the gruesome consequences. Dr Turner, Shelagh, Nurse Crane and Trixie deliver Margaret Lombardi's twins, which turns out to be a hazardous triplet birth. Violet holds a teddy bears' picnic to celebrate the birth of the Queen's baby, while Sister Monica Joan's disappearance with a fever leads to a desperate search.

EPISODE TWO

Lucille cares for Clarice Millgrove, a fiercely independent elderly hoarder living in filthy, condemned conditions. As Clarice's protests against eviction become more desperate, Lucille grows to respect the woman's suffragette past and her right to a dignified future. Elsewhere, Sister Hilda and Trixie care for expectant mother Flora Aidoo from Ghana, whose iron deficiency is discovered to be sickle cell anaemia, an inherited condition, with agonising consequences for her whole family. Meanwhile, Violet decides to run as a local councillor but is disheartened by Fred's lack of support.

EPISODE THREE

When extrovert mother of five Betty Marwick gives birth to a baby with a cleft lip and palate, she loses confidence in her mothering skills and Valerie must intervene to help, and to avoid baby Kirk's adoption. Uptake is slow for Dr Turner's local trial of a measles vaccine until Trixie's help and Teddy Turner's participation turn things around. Elsewhere, the Turners are troubled by new mum Hazel Becker's over-protectiveness of her daughter, until her past is revealed and she is able to find closure for her tragic loss. Meanwhile, Phyllis plans a unique bank holiday treat for the district by bringing the beach to Poplar.

EPISODE FOUR

Mother and daughter Enid Wilson and Cilla Singh are both pregnant but are not on speaking terms because of Cilla's marriage to Pardeep, a Sikh. Shelagh and Sister Julienne work tactfully to care for both until Cilla's life-threatening toxaemia gives a chance for reconciliation. Trixie and her Keep Fit group host a Keep Fit jamboree but group member and mother of two Jeannie Tennant is distressed to find herself pregnant again. When Dr Turner can't give her a legal abortion, Jeannie seeks a back-street solution – with devastating consequences. Meanwhile, Phyllis goes on an artistic date in Soho with Sergeant Woolf that turns out to be rather more radical than either expected.

EPISODE FIVE

Dr Turner, Shelagh and Trixie launch a new cervical screening clinic but a test on bride-to-be Lois Parry reveals that she possesses rare intersex characteristics. The revelation shatters her wedding plans and leads to an attempted suicide but a caring partner and family help her to adjust. Lucille hesitates about her feelings for handsome mechanic Cyril Robinson but ultimately agrees to go on a date with him. The husband of an expectant mother suffers with some inexplicable pains similar to his wife's pregnancy symptoms and Sister Frances has to conquer her fear of public speaking when she's assigned her first mothercraft class.

EPISODE SIX

Phyllis is hospitalised due to back trouble and the Nonnatuns are surprised when Mother Mildred arrives as a temporary replacement, eager to observe their work. Her blunt manner makes a disastrous start with the dock-working Britall family but when Barney Brittall contracts anthrax from cargo, Mother Mildred helps them fight for improved working conditions. An unmarried teenage mother refuses to give up her baby for adoption and Lucille must help her to face an uncertain future. Elsewhere, the Turners must steel themselves for May's impending adoption; Sister Monica Joan interferes with Lucille's budding romance and Valerie helps out her grandmother, Elsie Dyer, who is suffering from an embarrassing medical problem.

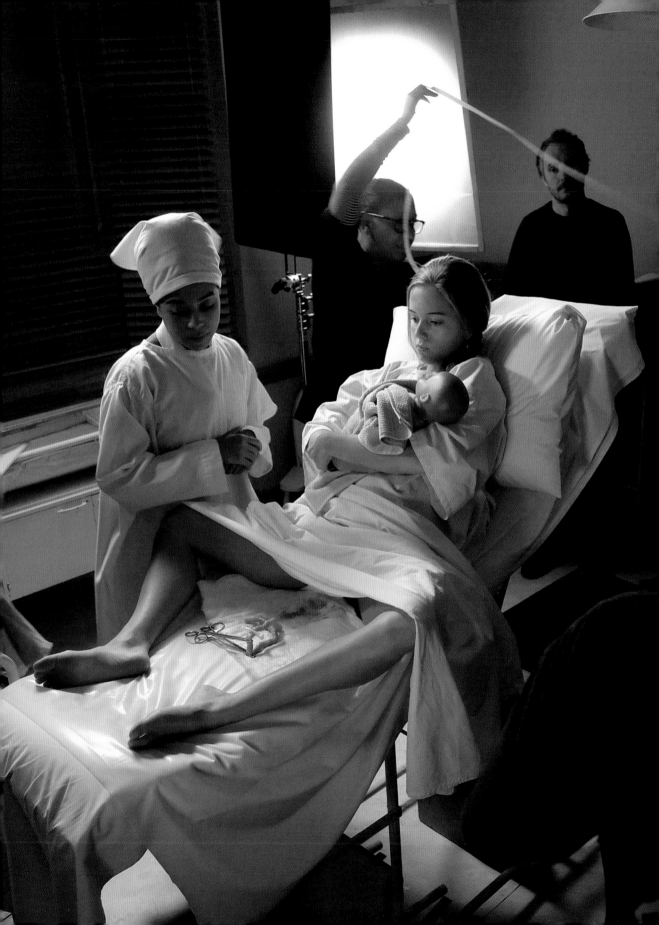

EPISODE SEVEN

Trixie is shocked when a young first-time mum Heather Pugh contracts gonorrhea due to her husband Vince's compulsion to visit prostitutes – with health implications for her unborn child. Dr Turner and Trixie campaign for a contraceptive advice clinic in Poplar but councillor Violet is unconvinced. Mother Mildred insists that Sister Frances must begin attending births unaccompanied, despite her lack of confidence. When help fails to show at the crucial moment, Frances digs deep and achieves a successful first solo delivery. But there's horror when Valerie answers a distress call from her gran, Elsie – and discovers that she's the one performing back-street abortions on vulnerable women.

EPISODE EIGHT

Valerie reports her grandmother to the police for illegal abortion and is forced to endure the agony of testifying against her in court. Elsie is initially defiant but when Cath (who suffered a botched abortion in episode one) gives evidence, Elsie changes her plea and is sentenced to prison. Shelagh distracts herself from May's impending adoption by organising a charity dance to raise money for an incubator for the maternity home. When teenager Julie Shroeder, a dying cancer patient, expresses the desire to attend, Sister Hilda is determined to do all she can to make her last dream a reality. Meanwhile, Phyllis plays cupid with Miss Higgins and Sergeant Woolf; Fred needs a prostate exam and Reggie is feeling lovesick.

CHRISTMAS 1964

The flu-stricken team head off to the Outer Hebrides to help out the local community with a gap in medical care. Sister Monica Joan is left behind but contrives a way to travel there herself on a personal pilgrimage of faith. Attempts to set up a clinic prove both a medical and cultural challenge. Phyllis and Trixie help Effie Tolmie, a teenager rebelling against the confining island lifestyle. Dr Turner performs a life-saving emergency appendectomy on a new mother in a remote lighthouse without electricity. Meanwhile, back in Poplar, Reggie attempts to set a record for the world's longest Christmas paper chain.

THE CRUCIBLE
OF COMPLEX
THINGS

Stephen McGann

Dr Turner

Watching Series Eight again was surprisingly moving. Surprising, because I'd assumed that having filmed it only a few years ago, I'd have an easy familiarity with the themes. A quick memory jog and I could breezily recount some pertinent detail. Yet the impact of it came back to me with a sickening thud.

This series, set in 1964, featured a multi-episodic exploration of abortion – still illegal in the United Kingdom at the time and a subject of increasing media and parliamentary debate. The Abortion Act of 1967, which set a new legal framework for termination, was still a few years off. Yet hospitals were dealing regularly with mutilated women who'd sought desperate measures for their unwanted pregnancy from word-of-mouth local fixers in filthy back rooms. Public outrage with the status quo was reaching its height. Change was needed, and change was coming. But not yet.

If there was any issue that typified the responsibility felt by *Call the*

Midwife for its subjects, then abortion was it. Not because there are simple truths to be told, but because there are not. Abortion is unpleasant. There's no context in which it is 'nice' or a trivial consideration for those involved. It's invariably born of crisis – a state of distress requiring urgent and life-affecting choices. There is no truth about abortion that isn't accompanied by some degree of pain, compromise or moral complexity.

Jennifer Worth, writer of the original *Call the Midwife* books, had seen the results of illegal abortion as a 1950s midwife and understood these grim complexities. Despite her personal faith, Jennifer was clear in her belief that abortion should be treated as a purely medical issue and not a moral one. 'A minority of women will always want an abortion. Therefore, it must be done properly.'

While a majority in the UK would probably share Jennifer's medical pragmatism, addressing the subject of pre-legal abortion 'properly' required more from *Call the Midwife* than a narrow focus on medical procedure. Drama is about human beings – their many conflicting emotions, beliefs and choices – and Series Eight was full of characters whose lives would be confronted in complex ways by the consequences of abortion. In episode one, there is a devastating sequence where would-be model Cath suffers the appalling aftermath of a botched abortion on the Nonnatus House bathroom floor. Sister Frances, inexperienced and traumatised, must clean up the mess. Cath's loving sister Leslie demands that the abortionist be brought to justice but Cath, her womb lost and her world altered, just wants to forget. Sister Julienne adopts Jennifer Worth's pragmatism, her morals challenged but her compassion resolute. Valerie is shocked but nevertheless hides Cath from Sergeant Woolf downstairs. All of those present are affected. All navigating their own difficult paths through the awful event.

It isn't long before Dr Turner is forced into his own terrible confrontation with abortion. Married mother of two Jeannie comes to him, pregnant again and pleading for a legal abortion – but Dr Turner can't grant her wish within the existing law. Jeannie then undergoes an illegal abortion that leaves her with a life-threatening infection. Dr Turner tries desperately to resuscitate Jeannie in an emergency ambulance dash to hospital but she dies – and Dr Turner is left with her husband's grief and anger, and his own guilt about what he didn't, or couldn't, do to help her.

I won't forget filming that scene in the ambulance. Ironically, like in the grim scene itself, we were badly running out of time. It was late in the day and we were left with only a few minutes to film it. The antique ambulance was driven into the studio and me and the excellent Molly Chesworth, who played Jeannie, were bundled into the back with our cramped camera crew. We were told to go for it straight away. I think that feeling of all-or-nothing urgency gave the scene a kind of energy. But seeing Molly lying there, slipping away like many desperate women had done, was motivation enough.

It's worth noting that many of the women seeking abortions at the time were mature and married with children. The common image of the 'immoral' single teen looking to escape the consequences of their actions is misleading. Jeannie had a family she loved. What killed her was wanting more control over it. That's the trouble with complexity – the worst consequences of it can be all too blunt and simple. We completed that scene in minutes but that blunt feeling stayed with me on the journey home, and ever since.

The series culminates in the cruellest of knife-twists for poor Valerie when she discovers that her own beloved gran Elsie is the back-street abortionist causing all of these infections. We knew that the actor playing her would have to carry an enormous amount of moral complexity in her performance. Elsie is of the street; hard-bitten but loving of her own; defiant in the face of the law but guided by her own moral code. I was therefore delighted when my friend Ann Mitchell took the part. She did it brilliantly – her final speech to Valerie as a convicted abortionist was full of bleak pragmatism and resignation, leaving Valerie to navigate her own difficult actions and feelings.

No character comes out of Series Eight unscarred by these events. And that's as it should be. There's no simple answer to the challenges presented because abortion is not simple. Our characters are left to do what they believe is most right, without the satisfaction of it feeling easy, or clean, or nice, or comfortable. And in that way, they touch a deeper wisdom about drama, life and the laws we all live by.

Our society shows its best face when it has the courage to do what's most good for most people in circumstances that can never feel wholly easy. Drama, likewise, thrives best when it has the courage to exist in that same crucible of complex things, where answers can't be perfect, painless or simple but where questions must still be addressed with compassion and humility.

ELLA AND FENELLA

Ella Bruccoleri

Sister Frances

I was so lucky to join the cast at the same time as Fenella – we've practically got the same name so we sort of homogenised and she has become a really good confidante and friend. She's an artist and she's got a lot of experience, whereas I was just a few months out of drama school, and we held each other's hands – in fact, we still do in a way. I can't express how much she's helped me, not only with career advice but on a personal level. She's very good at knowing when you're at a stage that she might have found difficult herself and giving you a piece of advice that just hits the nail on the head.

I was also lucky in that I was able to build my nerves into the way I played the character. It took me a while to warm up and allow my true personality to come out and it wasn't until my third series that I felt really comfortable. You don't have much time to get into the character and I was told I'd got the part only a few days before we started filming so I was finding my way in front of the camera. It does take time – I'm not sure I know myself, let alone Sister Frances! But what's great about being on a long-running show is that you can delve deep.

My original contract was for three years so I knew that it was

ongoing for at least that period. Sister Frances is beginning to show different sides to her – she's a loving, kind, very religious and quite timid person but she's got a real temper. I've enjoyed exploring that. And sometimes she's very funny, although not usually intentionally – it's just that she has no filter. There's a scene where she has a wonderful line when a delivery arrives for Trixie. Sister Frances looks at it and says, 'What kind of man would give a woman a cheese plant?'

Fenella Woolgar

Sister Hilda

I read Jennifer Worth's books in preparation and they're startlingly unsentimental. My husband is a doctor, trained at Barts and the Royal London in the East End, and he was really struck by that when I read sections out to him. She tells it like it was – the stench and the grime and the poverty. We've got further away from that as the series has progressed and we've moved into the 1960s with improved social conditions, up to a point at least, but at the start it was so important that the world on screen was true to that, not scrubbed or sanitised.

It was fun when I joined to be a big Sister – literally! – to Ella as Sister Frances. And I've loved the feeling that Sister Hilda has quite a glamorous past. She's definitely not a retiring wallflower and she likes being in charge but alongside that she's sensitive to personal pain and to what people are going through. There's not a snobbish bone in her body. I might possibly over-pride myself in my lack of vanity but in some respects I've definitely lucked out in being a nun. We're in and out of make-up in five minutes, no tweaking when we're ready to shoot, no lipstick to adjust and no 5 a.m. pick-up followed by hours with your hair in hot rollers. None of that. What I don't get to take advantage of is the fact that I've had children myself, so that bit I do know about. I do love babies so it's been a joy to have tiny ones around – mine are beyond that stage.

When you join a long-running show you do hope that you'll be in it for enough time to get a chance to develop your character. You never know what might be written for you or what aspect of your character's past might come up. Of course, when you first meet someone they're not necessarily the person that they might reveal themselves to be over time. They might inadvertently be giving a different idea of themselves through nerves or anxiety, or determination to make a good impression. The more you get to do, the more rewarding it is, and I love having that opportunity to show many aspects of myself.

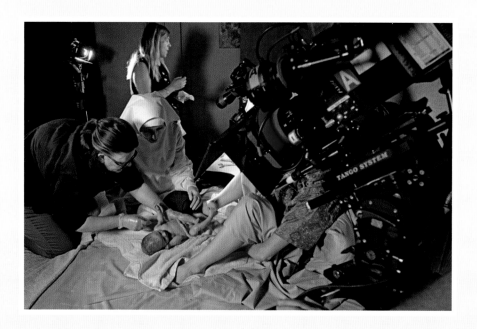

SECRET SHAME

Jennifer Kirby

Valerie Dyer

Call the Midwife has made me more aware of social issues. Most actors are sensitive in that you have to let things in and allow yourself to be affected by stories, but then you have to put that to one side in order to perform. The way that the stories are constructed is always brilliant and you get a perspective on things that you might have thought about but about which you certainly haven't comprehended the full reality. The story about back-street abortions was one of those – and it was shocking to be reminded of how recent it all was. Ann Mitchell, playing my grandmother Elsie, had a direct link to that world. She's from Stepney and was brought up mostly by female relatives. She was amazing in every respect, both in terms of having had that first-hand lived experience and also in terms of being an actress of such experience. It was a privilege to work so closely with her and to hear her stories of women who hid their pregnancies and tried to terminate them, their fear and the feelings of shame they had to put up with. The storyline of Valerie discovering that Elsie was responsible for women's deaths because of carrying out illegal abortions was incredibly challenging and very rewarding to play.

Ann Mitchell

Elsie Dyer

———

I am a proper East Ender, born in Stepney. My grandfather was a docker and when he was thirty-five he came home on a Friday evening not feeling well and he was dead of pneumonia on the Monday morning. It was so quick, and there were no antibiotics. I imagine that he was very fearful of not being able to get to work on the Monday because the family depended on him. My grandmother was left with three children, pregnant with my mother, and no husband. Neighbours and other family members all rallied round to help and the children had to look out for one another, which was still the case by the time I was growing up. We'd be playing out on the street most of the day. I've got a scar on the back of my right leg from sliding down a mound on a bomb site and cutting myself on broken glass.

I was a fan of the series before I was asked to play Elsie Dyer and I was incredibly impressed by how authentic and radical it was. The issues that were dealt with were very important and it really did represent the atmosphere and the moral, ethical code that so many people lived by in the East End. Heidi Thomas wrote the role for me, which was thrilling. Her own personality comes out in the writing, which is skilful, not at all sentimental and very tough. The issues that she addresses are subtly filtered in and balanced with the lives and stories of the nuns and midwives. I'm fascinated by the portrayal of midwifery and how that changed – it went from being quite upper-class to working class. In Poplar and Stepney Green they were absolutely essential; people wouldn't have been able to manage without those strong women in a community, delivering babies.

Elsie is a properly nuanced, complicated character. She is presented in all her contradictory dimensions and complexity and not simply as a caricature of a wicked old crone wielding a pair of rusty knitting needles. And she looked formidable; she gave off a strong sense of respectability and dignity. Those iron-grey curls – they were a bit like a helmet, her personal armour. When she was confronted by Val, her own granddaughter, you might have expected her to collapse in shame at what she's done but she fights back. She believes very strongly that she is performing an essential service. It was an intolerable situation for women before birth control and very well known in the East End. You couldn't be seen to have an illegitimate child and women who were desperately poor and already had three or four children couldn't afford to have another.

Getting it right was a huge responsibility. There are still people alive who lived that experience and they could be watching with a very jaundiced eye. It was always real and it was never patronising and that was so important. The show has a strong cast of women, which I loved – particularly because all the women were working in one way or another. That was great to see. In my experience of being brought up in Stepney, all the women I knew worked – they had to.

I was gutted when it came to an end – I hated being killed off! I remember saying, 'Isn't there any way I could come back?' I came up with a whole storyline for Elsie in which she has an epiphany in prison and gets religion. Then I could have come back as a nun!

Jenny Agutter

Sister Julienne

Sister Julienne is having to do the best work she can in a world that's constantly changing. There was an episode when you saw into her past, how she could have gone another way, could have married, but she has no regrets about that. She's made her choices and made them very particularly, with huge commitment. She is dedicated to her faith and to the community and I think that nothing else matters to her, so if she's dealing with someone whose morals she may not approve of, she doesn't even think about that – she just takes care of the person. She makes absolutely no judgements – that's out of her remit. It's an enormous source of strength for her because she knows her way. She's there to serve, particularly the women and children. It was immensely shocking for her when she found the baby with thalidomide who'd been left to die but once she recognised that there was no way it was going to survive, everything came into focus for her – all she had to do was take care of that child's life until it was over.

When she has to deal with a woman miscarrying because of an

attempt to abort her child it's the same – she makes no judgement. She's there to look after the woman and, if necessary, to mop up the mess. She's also a very good listener; she'll listen to everybody, to whatever they have to say, and she finds what people have to say not just interesting but really important. One's always aware, for example, that Sister Monica Joan is out there with the fairies sometimes and that her mind is not necessarily on the practicalities, but her wisdom comes through and the insight that she has to aspects of life are very good for Sister Julienne. A convent is full of many different types of women and she has to deal with them all.

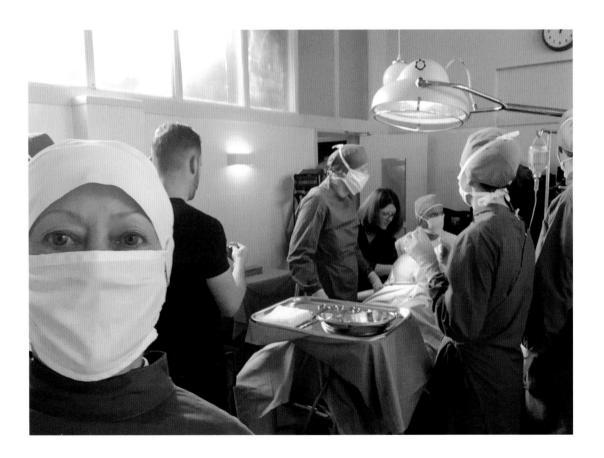

MORE THAN A MECHANIC

Zephryn Taitte

Cyril Robinson

It's quite special to play a really good man who has a depth and an edge to him as well. When I started, I was going for innocent, sincere and vulnerable – then he got more confident and I could develop a cheekier, more charming side to him. I think I had four episodes for certain and it wasn't definite that I'd be going on for more than that, but then it just took off, which was wonderful. People really liked the relationship between Cyril and Lucille.

From the moment I stepped onto the set, there were smiles, welcomes all round – it felt like a big family and I was the big kid. I'd been to LA a few months before and I went on a tour of Universal Studios, saw Steven Spielberg's office, the backlots, everything, and I was completely fascinated. I had the same reaction on *Call the Midwife* – asking tons of questions, wanting to know what everyone did, what all the bits of kit were. SO geeky! I expect I really annoyed everyone, especially Leonie. I was like a giddy child with the costume department, trying things on, getting them to take pictures. And I get to wear some really cool stuff. I think it was the first day when I was told I had to ride a motorbike, a really old-school one with a sidecar. I thought, 'Throw me in at the deep end, why don't you?' But I went for it and it was all right.

What I didn't see coming was that Cyril would be a godly man. Sister Monica Joan encourages his spiritual aspect, shifting him towards being a carer in the community, feeling a sense of responsibility. And because he falls in love with Lucille it makes him want to fix himself up, be more presentable, show a deeper side to himself as well as being a mechanic. There's a line where he says, 'I thought I was coming here to fix things, but now I'm fixing people' – I loved that.

HATS AND BRAS AND PINK GINGHAM

Claire Lynch

Costume designer, Series 8 – 10

It was 1963/4 on the series when I joined so it was a really interesting period. I love finding out what happened historically in a particular year and how that affected what people wore. You learn so much from research, from looking at photographs – in the early sixties, older men would still almost always wear hats but younger men had started to go bareheaded. Women would wear hats for church and Miss Higgins, in her role as receptionist at the surgery and the maternity home, helping out the Turners, is old-fashioned and formal so she wears a hat to work. I talked to Georgie Glen, who plays her, and we decided that it should be a slightly military-looking beret. And she's not got a lot of money so she wears the same suits and blouses, which she looks after very carefully. Underwear is important because it has such an effect on people's outline, their shape. Luckily, the 1960s Gossard bra was very much the same shape as a modern-day M&S T-shirt bra – they'd moved on from the pointed shape of the 1950s. In October 1964, Biba opened in

London and that was hugely influential for young women. Barbara Hulanicki, who started Biba, designed a pink gingham dress in the May of that year and it was featured in the *Daily Mirror*. Within days she'd got over 4,000 orders. It was a galloping success so we recreated it for Valerie Dyer to wear. That was fun.

Of course, the chief person for fashion is Trixie and we do allow her a bit of a get-out clause with new outfits because of her getting a dress allowance from her godmother in Portofino, this wonderful character who's referred to but never appears. In fact, Helen and I have invented a whole personality for her and we've decided that if she ever turns up she definitely has to be played by Joanna Lumley. When I started, in Series Eight, Helen was coming back after having her baby so I wanted to make sure she had a pretty spectacular outfit for that. I'd found an image of this beautiful Givenchy coat so we modified it a bit – it had a really high neck that we had to change – and created a design around that, trying lots of different colours on her until we knew what tone we wanted. Luckily, she and I are about the same size so I can use myself as a rough model, trying on the toiles – the prototype version of garments that you make to get the fit right before using the real fabric.

We make and buy a lot of the clothes for the regular principal actors – I have a list of trusted vintage sellers – and hire them for guest actors from Angels, which is like a vast warehouse for vintage clothes, divided into different sections. I really couldn't manage without it but I have to remember what I've used before. Woe betide us if a dress comes back on another person! Fortunately, I have quite a photographic memory of what I've used and also extensive albums and folders on my iPad.

At the end of 1963, my muses for the Turners were JFK and Jackie Kennedy. Shelagh was doing more admin then, less midwifery, so she needed a few professional suits. And she was a working mother so her clothes needed to be practical. I put her in trousers for the first time – there was an outcry on Twitter! – and gave her nice knitwear, a silk scarf knotted round her neck. I had to get a few things made for her because Laura's so petite. We livened the colour up a bit too. In the back of everyone's garments we sew little silk labels and the character's name.

The hardest clothes to get right are actually the ones that need to look bad. Sometimes with vintage clothes you don't need to do too much work on them but often, so that something looks right on a character who's very poor, they have to be completely broken down. And although in real life you might find three people together all wearing a slightly different green jumper, on screen it would look ridiculous so we make sure that doesn't happen.

THE DEVIL'S IN
THE DETAIL

Annie Tricklebank

Producer, Series 4–10

My route into producing was via all sorts of different jobs – research, production management, script editing, line producing. In order to be a decent producer, you need to know exactly what everybody else does. You need to support them but sometimes you need to challenge them, to confront what they do. There can be a hundred different people working on a film crew at any one time – construction workers, props people, make-up, costume – and you need to relate to them, to walk with all of them. Your work can't just be focused on the script and the actors. The tiniest thing that's wrong can be picked up. Of course, the medical research and detail has to be spot on but it's other things as well, like the colour of someone's lipstick.

Voices are crucial and some of the actors bring something that's an enhanced version of their own voice to their characters on *Call the Midwife* – Annabelle Apsion speaks more slowly as Violet and has a sort of twang, a flatness. Cliff sounds even juicier as Fred than as himself; Judy Parfitt is slower, more gracious and ruminative, slightly fey, as Sister Monica Joan. Heidi knows the voices so well that the lines she writes are always perfect, exactly right for them.

Locations are very bonding – we had a wonderful time on Lewis and Harris for the Series Eight Christmas special, even though the Hebridean weather was wild and the logistics were fairly hair-raising. It was incredibly beautiful and we were made so welcome by the local community.

HEBRIDES

Reza Eftekhari

Transport captain

I was just a unit driver on the first three series but then I got promoted. There's a lot of different elements to organise – sixteen-seater minibuses for the crew, cars for the actors, checking on traffic delays. Before the pandemic I could have three artists in the same car, so Fenella Woolgar, Jenny Agutter and Laura Main would often share because they live not far from one another. Sometimes they chat, sometimes they catch up on emails and phone calls, and if they need to get some sleep they can doze.

I'm based in Bromley so I often drive the cast members who are south London based. I've got a people carrier and sometimes it can get quite full. When there's a baby with parents, and sometimes brothers and sisters, as soon as others get to hear about it, their nan says she'd like to come too and they can end up with quite an entourage. Annie Tricklebank is brilliant – she just trusts me to do what's necessary. On a busy day I must be first in and last out, starting early and leaving late. I have to keep tabs on everything, to be very on the ball, following the scene orders, making sure I'm told if they change so that actors have different release times.

The Outer Hebrides was a challenge! We went on a four-day recce but when our usual drivers got there and saw the terrain – single tracks, having to give way all the time – a lot of them didn't feel happy about driving there. I had to think fast. There was a man on Harris who hired me four minibuses with drivers but because the island's so small they all knew each other and they were running other jobs at the same time – they were fishermen, post office workers – and they weren't always available when I needed them. So on the first weekend I was knocking on doors anywhere that I saw minibuses parked in front of the house and asking to employ the owners. But it was half term and they were either doing runs, taking the elderly to the supermarket, or they didn't want to work. I had to find drivers who knew the island because sat nav didn't help – at one stage, we had a location to get to and we were just given a postcode. It was a road about seven and a half miles long and one driver thought after three and a half miles that it just couldn't be right so he turned round and came back. All the journeys were a minimum of an hour each way. It wasn't the mileage that was the problem, so much as the road surface and the conditions.

Linda Bassett

Phyllis Crane

I loved the Hebrides. We were shooting in a village one day and some of the local women had been gathered for us to film them 'waulking' the Harris tweed. It's the last stage in the long process of making it. You sit round a large table and you rub the tweed and pull it and rub it and pull it. It softens and strengthens it I think. It was something I had learned about years ago when I worked in Theatre in Education. I asked their permission to go in and watch and they invited me to join in, which was thrilling. They always sing as they work and I joined in with that too. Very satisfying.

Miriam Margolyes

Mother Mildred

Wearing a habit is a complex matter – it's a very difficult thing to do, to get dressed as a nun. There are many different garments. Not just the wimple, which is a trial all of its own. When we were filming the Christmas episode on the Isle of Harris, the weather was absolutely brutal, lashing rain and wind, and to have a dripping wimple is something I wouldn't wish on anybody. Nonetheless, it was so beautiful that I long to return. And the episode was a triumph, a very good one.

Helen George

Trixie Franklin

It was so cold! I don't think I got warm for a month after that shoot.

SERIES NINE

1 9 6 5

EPISODE ONE

Fred finds a newborn baby abandoned in a dustbin and a search begins for her mother. She is discovered to be a Catholic priest's housekeeper – and when the priest's keenness for the child's adoption hints at his own part in it an angry Mother Mildred takes mother and child back to the Mother House. Phyllis helps an expectant mother and son move from a filthy homeless shelter to a council flat but the boy later falls sick with deadly diphtheria. Dr Turner traces the local outbreak to the shelter where they'd stayed. Valerie patches up relations with her cousin Maureen Bryant after her grandmother's imprisonment, while Sister Julienne finds out that Nonnatus House is earmarked for demolition.

EPISODE TWO

Pregnant Laverne Bulmer's middle-aged mum and babysitter Florrie Watkins develops liver disease and memory loss, leading to suspicions of alcoholic neglect. But Dr Turner identifies the cause as serious but treatable haemochromatosis. When lively but struggling local prostitute Tina Atkins is endangered by an ectopic pregnancy, Sister Julienne is determined to help her get her life back on track. But Tina's previous children are discovered in care, revealing her life story as a fantasy and Sister Julienne accepts that Tina cannot be changed. Sister Hilda is recruited as a school nit nurse, while Sergeant Woolf's heart attack causes him to terminate his relationship with a forlorn Miss Higgins.

EPISODE THREE

Lucille is seconded to St Cuthbert's to supervise student midwives but experiences prejudice from pregnant patient Connie Blair. Lucille's skilful handling of Connie's attitude and insecurities, and her eventful labour in a trapped hospital lift, bring belated respect. Phyllis's concern for two Sylheti schoolboys leads her to discover their suffering mother, Farzina Mohammed, abandoned by her husband due to a lingering childbirth injury. Dr Turner helps diagnose a surgically treatable fistula, while Phyllis encourages Farzina's husband to return to them. The midwives stage a grand fashion show to raise money for an incubator.

EPISODE FOUR

Sister Julienne agrees to house and supervise four male trainee doctors for a week but Nurse Crane is sceptical. Benedict Walters is talented but proves disruptive, causing friction with the Sisters. Valerie helps working-class Kevin McNulty cope with a difficult first birth. The week ultimately proves a success. Elsewhere, Fred and Reggie befriend George Benson, a reclusive old pigeon keeper living in a condemned property nearby. Reggie and George bond over the birds but there's alarm when George collapses, coughing blood. Dr Turner is mystified when TB tests are negative; however, trainee Kevin identifies a rare lung condition related to the pigeons George keeps. George recovers, is rehoused and Fred helps bring him back into the community.

EPISODE FIVE

Stressed matriarch Grace Calthorpe is driven to despair by the demands of her needy family but when Sister Julienne reaches out, she's accused of being out of touch with real life. When Grace ends up in hospital, Sister Frances instigates a new family regime to help her. But Grace's remarks lead Sister Julienne to venture out into Poplar without her habit, to sample life outside Nonnatus walls.

Timothy wins tickets to see *The Sound of Music* in a raffle and persuades his overworked parents to go on a romantic date. Phyllis struggles with nervous dad Ronald Mallen, who insists on attending the birth and panics at the sight of the baby's birth mark. Sister Hilda eventually unlocks the past family pains driving Ronald's parental insecurity.

EPISODE SIX

The Turners' plans to adopt May are rocked when May's birth mother, Esther Tang, thought dead, seeks renewed contact with her daughter. A meeting proves traumatic and Sister Julienne attempts to mediate but the Turners must accept uncertainty over May's long-term status. Valerie's cousin Maureen gives birth to a boy but tragedy strikes when the child dies from complications due to rubella contracted by Maureen. Trainee doctor Kevin is taken on as a GP at the surgery but his liberal dispensing practices unsettle Sister Frances. Fred and Reggie organise a horticultural show, which Sister Monica Joan wins with a creative interpretation of a flower display.

EPISODE SEVEN

Trixie is worried for expectant mum Marion Irmsby, who is blind but determined to care for her new child independently. With Trixie's support and following reconciliation with her sister, Marion learns her limits and finds the help she needs. Pregnant mother Yvonne Smith's respite in the maternity home is shattered by her abusive husband. Kevin expels him but the new doctor's pethidine abuse becomes clear, and his unnecessary intervention in Yvonne's birth to appropriate her pain relief alarms Sister Frances. Valerie visits her gran in prison and becomes concerned for her health, while Lucille, Cyril and Fred help Phyllis with a new Cubs go-kart building project.

EPISODE EIGHT

When the council reduces crucial funding for Nonnatus House, the end looks near for the team. With little time to put their case, a local petition is organised. Trixie gives an impassioned speech in defence of their work and they win a limited reprieve. When Valerie's gran is diagnosed with terminal cancer, she is released into Valerie's care and her moving death brings remorse and reconciliation. Kevin's drug problem is finally exposed and his medical future looks bleak. When two young mothers in the maternity home turn out to be pregnant by the same man, Phyllis needs all of her skill to keep the peace and find a way forward.

CHRISTMAS 1965

When the circus comes to Poplar, a fire forces pregnant trapeze artiste Jacquetta Ellings to give birth in the Black Sail pub, while Phyllis helps her circus-owner father to confront his approaching death from cancer, and his daughter's non-circus future. Shelagh is reunited with

Gloria Venables from Series Six – pregnant again, but at risk of miscarriage once more. She helps her old friend reconcile with her past losses and she finally gives birth to a perfect daughter. Trixie joins a marriage bureau with unfortunate results; the Buckles have a new shop and when Sister Monica Joan has a fall, she faces a hospitalised Christmas, until rescued at the last minute by Lucille.

NEVER WORK
WITH ANIMALS
OR CHILDREN

Stephen McGann

Dr Turner

'How's fake son doing, Dad?'

My son Dominic is home from university. He's asking after Max Macmillan, who plays Timothy Turner – my 'fake' screen son. Max is now at university himself. He's doing well, I tell Dominic. 'Send him my regards,' says Dom with a grin. When I tell Max on set later, he smiles too. 'Give my regards back to real son.'

They've been doing this for years, although they've never actually met. And I love it. Dom's a few years older than Max but near enough in age to remember how those milestones feel. Both of them take an amused and friendly interest in the existence of the other. And both mark a touching intersection in my own life. Two families that currently define me: one real, one played out in fiction for the world.

The Turner family is a rare privilege. A drama family that I've been allowed to grow with on TV for ten years. A functional, loving family – that has the same kind of hopes and dreams as many real families

out there. A family that has crises and challenges, but the same sweet landmarks, too. Birthdays. Christmases. Parties and evening meals. As any parent knows, there's a particular joy in watching the kids grow up in front of you – even if those kids are just actors in the same drama, rather than your own flesh and blood. Laura and I feel like very proud (fake) parents!

The wry undergraduate Max who now shares off-camera banter with me is that same Max who appeared in our first Christmas special in 2012 as a Cub Scout! And our lovely Alice Brown, who plays adopted Angela Turner, has been playing that part in *Call the Midwife* since she was quite literally a babe in arms. She recently told me on set (very proudly) that she's going to be eight years old this year. Eight years of watching this lovely child grow up with us, learning to speak – and now even saying her own lines!

This continuity has been such a bonus for us and something I think has really helped to fuse the Turners into a bonded screen family. It was certainly never a foregone conclusion. The rules about when and how one can employ child actors on screen are, quite rightly, very strict. Productions like ours must work around schoolwork, exams and holidays, but most of all, around the child's wishes. Every year, we asked each child if they'd like to return. And every year we were delighted that they did. We were the lucky ones.

But of course, Tim and Angela aren't the only children in the growing Turner family. By Series Nine, we'd acquired two more! Our youngest member is Teddy, the child that Shelagh gave birth to in Series Six. He's played by the cool and sassy Ned Shaw. Ned is an absolute hoot! Our second daughter May, played by the wonderful April Rae Hoang, had her own moving journey to make in the drama of Series Nine, when she undergoes a tug-of-love crisis involving her birth mother that rips into the family's happiness and peace.

April's introduction to the Turners began in the Christmas special of 1963, when May came over to England with Sister Mildred as part of the Hong Kong adoption programme. Series Nine was April's second complete series with us. We were immediately impressed by her ability to play the loneliness and loss of May at such a young age; she was remarkably self-aware and still in a scene, and then, as soon as the cameras cut, she would snap out of it and be her bright little self again. It gave us an added emotional tool for the scenes we needed in Series Nine, when Patrick and Shelagh confront the sudden reappearance of May's birth mother Esther, who was thought to have died. For a child under six to be able to play those confused emotions in these scenes was quite something.

Yet for all the good dramatic reasons for casting April, there was also a rather tender personal motive that encouraged Heidi to introduce the character of May in the way she did – which is an indicator of the way *Call the Midwife* thinks and cares about its own. Heidi had thought it would be nice for Alice to have a friend on set – someone that she could talk to and play with on those long filming days.

Can you imagine how long and boring those days must feel for a young child? Strange adults barging around with their equipment – all the lights and noises? And those endless hours of waiting. Our Alice had grown up with chaperones to entertain her and two lovely parents to look after her but Heidi thought that if the girls had someone of their own age to spend time with it would be far more rewarding for both children. And so it proved. The girls hit it off straight away – and to see them laughing together on set makes the heart sing. When Ned joins them it's a formidable family unit! The three kids now arrive on the Turner set like a whirlwind of smiles and energy. Oh, and rabbits – we now have a hutch on our Turner patio and the children periodically release the bunnies to run around the place in proper chaotic family fashion.

You know that old film cliché about never working with animals and children? Nonsense. I've spent a good portion of my life on *Call the Midwife* working with both and I can tell you that it's balm for the soul. Having children and babies on set is a constant reminder that there is always someone more important than you in the room and something far more important in life than just making television. These little future adults – like Max before them – are laying down memories and feelings for a life beyond you. To watch them grow, and think, and laugh, and dream in one's company is a gift. As a parent, I've been humbled by that process in my own son. As an actor, I've been lucky to have had a large pretend family to be humbled by as the years roll on.

Drama's power to represent doesn't preclude an actor's chance for vicarious joy. The things grown in stories of the heart become real in their sincere telling. The family might be 'fake' but my affection for them all is 100 per cent genuine.

TEARS AND SMILES

Laura Main

Shelagh Turner

I love the days with the kids, I really do. They're getting easier and easier as they grow up a bit. Max was eleven when he first appeared as Timothy Turner and I can hardly believe now how little he was when he joined the show. He's always been a brilliant performer and great to be around but now we're working with an adult! With Alice/Angela, I can remember moments when some coaxing was needed, occasional tears. She and April/May have a real connection. What's nice is you've got less time to worry about yourself; you're totally focused on trying to make the child happy and comfortable. Ned, who plays Teddy, is pretty much himself as a character and because the other children are a bit older, it's almost like a ready-made playgroup for him. I do recall a scene that was proving difficult and I was standing by – I wasn't even in it but I said, 'What if we all start singing "Row, row, row your boat"' – and we all did, including the crew. That worked! You become almost an assistant director on those days and, after all, Stephen and I are the ones who know them best. The directors and assistant directors come and go but we're always there. We know what they'll be up for doing and what they might find more difficult.

The wonderful thing about Heidi's writing is how well she knows us, so there are things that feel like coming home, that are familiar in a good way, and then you'll find yourself doing something that comes from a completely different angle and takes you into new territory. There are still different dynamics to play between Shelagh and Patrick and, looking back, both Stephen and I realise how instrumental Max as Timothy was in that connection, rolling his eyes when he thinks they're being a bit lovey-dovey. The relationship between Shelagh and Timothy is so nice too, cemented early on by the polio story.

Max Macmillan

Timothy Turner

I'm the middle one in my family – I've got an older sister and a younger brother – so it's not like the Turner set-up at all. It's always a fun day of shooting when the little ones are on set, with everyone making an extra effort to make sure they're happy. When they were really young, I remember we had to have scenes cut and there were difficult days when everyone would have their heads in their hands, trying to get a crucial shot. But now they've grown up a bit they have an absolute blast. Laura has worked her magic and Stephen's like a clown on set, making them laugh. I think he misses his own son being that age.

Miriam Margolyes

Mother Mildred

When Sister Mildred pitched up at Nonnatus House with a bunch of children in tow she'd clearly been in China for a long time and really knew the sadness of foundlings. I think she may have been based on a real person in Hong Kong who brought children over to England. I find working with children quite a challenge. May, who plays the child that the Turners end up adopting, is terrifically good and quite a character. I don't think she likes me very much, though.

NEW GIRLS TOGETHER

Jennifer Kirby

Valerie Dyer

Leonie joined the Nonnatus team not long after I did so we were new girls at the same time – that was really nice. We got on and have a similar way of working, making a lot of notes. We're both quite nerdy actors, I think; we like to talk about who might be feeling what at any given time and that informed the way we both played our characters initially. One thing that's brilliant about Heidi, and all the writers, is that they take a certain amount of lead from the way we perform the parts. Leonie and I had a connection and our characters did as well. In my last episode on the show, when Valerie's grandmother Elsie was dying, there was a bit where Lucille was helping and I remember feeling really grateful for that because it was a sort of closure for us as characters. It was perfectly orchestrated and spoke volumes. The characters never say, 'That's my best friend,' but it emerges – their affection for each other is shown through their actions. Being with somebody when their close relative is dying is one of the best things you can do for a person, the most loving.

Georgie Glen

Miss Millicent Higgins

I'm what's called a semi-regular on *Call the Midwife*, which is thrilling, as when I started I thought it was for one episode only. They tread carefully with new characters to see how they fit into the greater scheme of things. Annie Tricklebank gave odd hints that maybe my character could be developed and I hardly dared hope as it was beyond my wildest dreams, really, to be a part of an ongoing show, and this one of all shows – for the first time ever my mother was impressed!

In fact, my mother is a helpful role model for Miss Higgins – in the 1960s she dressed in a very similar way. We lived in Helensburgh and Tuesday was when she went to Glasgow, usually taking me with her, which must have been annoying. She always wore a suit and a hat and gloves, and we'd have lunch at Fullers, very respectable, very familiar and comforting. Miss Higgins is a product of her time and her upbringing – proper but not prim.

You have to extract all the information you can from the script and make sure that your core character is firmly embedded – then you can accommodate a curve ball coming your way from Heidi, who's a great one for springing surprises. I need to know who I am as Miss Higgins so if I suddenly reveal an eccentric interest, like having taken part in a Charleston competition in 1926, it can come over as startling but not completely implausible. There's always a slight twinkle and wickedness, though nobody sees that apart from Nurse Crane, who looks beyond the fierce efficiency and stiff upper lip, and sees that there's a seething mass of fun and passion underneath. She'd probably have been an excellent teacher – she likes young people, she's interested in them, even if she's not used to them. Every now and again she has a little moment with Reggie Jackson or Timothy Turner.

All of that is expressed through her clothes, so our costume designer, Claire Lynch, has said to me, 'I don't want you to think I'm being negligent but I think Miss Higgins should keep the suits she has. She's careful and economical and has good-quality suits that she repairs and looks after extremely carefully.' It's her uniform, her armour. I must say, if she ever does go on holiday with Nurse Crane I'll be interested to see what she wears on the beach.

That friendship between the two women is beautifully done – it's a nice strand for women of that age to befriend each other. They're both single and the label of 'spinster' in those days was such a dismissive one. And I like their differences – they both read poetry but Phyllis likes Lorca while Millicent goes for Patience Strong. It was delicious to play the scene where they sigh over the inevitability of being given bath cubes for Christmas. And their choice of the perfect indulgent meal: baked beans on toast for Phyllis but for Millicent a simply enormous bowl of trifle washed down with a Harvey Wallbanger!

LUCILLE

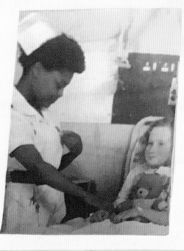

PHOTO OF A WEST INDIAN HAIR SALON -
BUT THEY WERE FEW AND FAR BETWEEN.
MOST LADIES STYLED THEIR HAIR AT
HOME.
TO STRAIGHTEN OR PRESS THE HAIR AN
IRON COMB WOULD BE USED OFTEN
HEATED UP ON THE RINGS OF A GAS
FIRE.
HAIR WAS THEN SET ON SPONGE
ROLLERS THEN STYLED.
A FINE SCARF WAS WORN IN BED TO PROTECT
ROLLERS/STYLE

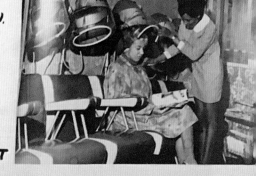

IN SOME PHOTOS WIGS AR
BEING WORN BY POPULAR
SINGER OF THE DAY. THES

HIGHLIGHTS
AND EYELINER

Stella O'Farrell

Hair and make-up supervisor, Series 4–10

At one time in film and television, hair and make-up were different departments but on most productions now they're together. I create a mood board for each character and try to give them a bit of a backstory. So with Lucille, for example, I looked at young women of around her age and how they were doing their hair and I found a picture of a salon that was the sort of place she might have gone to.

We can't always give everyone the most up-to-date look because most people would still have had hairdos from a few years earlier. It has to look as if they could manage it by themselves so we'll do their hair and then undo it a bit. People did take a lot of effort with their hair in the 1960s – lots of lacquer and backcombing. If an actress has very fine, straight hair we ask them not to wash it for a couple of days, then the styles take a lot better and stay in a lot better as well. Coloured hair would have looked very flat at the time so we're always keen to get hold of the new cast members as soon as possible as so many women have highlights now and they didn't have them then. Over the years, we've worked with a lovely colourist at the Charles Worthington salon in London; actresses get a colour wash put over their highlights, then, after we've finished filming all their

scenes, we'll pay for them to have their highlights reinstated. During the pandemic, we weren't able to do that but then people weren't able to keep their highlights going either so that cancelled out that worry. With actresses who have a birth sequence to perform, we work out how their hairstyle would break down to look realistic.

Certain things were really popular and much copied. In 1963, when the film *Cleopatra* came out, Revlon did a massive advertising campaign for Cleopatra eyes and we decided that was definitely something that Trixie would have had a go at. There was a lipstick to go with it called Sphinx Pink! By 1966, Twiggy was the face of fashion and she had those painted-on eyelashes but they'd have been a bit over the top for a working midwife.

It's not just how the make-up looks on people's faces, it's the make-up they might use on screen. We can provide them with a vintage powder compact, for example, but it wouldn't be filled with vintage powder. And lipstick cases used to be a lot narrower so I've got a stash of a particular one from Boots that looks right once we take the outer label off. Then there's 'no make-up' make-up for the nuns, which makes their preparation time a lot shorter. Some poor folk are being seen to for quite a while.

Teeth can be tricky because most people's teeth are so much whiter now than they used to be. In Series Six, we had a character who had very bad teeth. She had to have them all pulled out and dentures put in but she went into labour as she was having the teeth pulled. We worked with this brilliant man called Chris Lyons who made a set of gums for her that covered her own teeth and had a dentist on hand to advise us so that a shot of one tooth being extracted was exactly the right one.

SHARED
PROBLEMS

Annie Tricklebank

Producer, Series 4–10

I love working on *Call the Midwife* because I love the writing, the actors, the crew and most of all, because of the world we present, its complete sense of reality. People ask whether some of the stories make me angry. Of course they do, but we can reach people who, as a result of watching the programme, might even respond by making changes for the better themselves. So much is covered in each episode – different ethnicities and cultures and religions. We may be covering a time period more than fifty years ago but, unfortunately, some things haven't changed – people still live in poverty, people are still out of work, living on the streets, not able to get to a doctor. I was talking to Vanessa Redgrave recently, when we were recording her voiceovers, and she said, 'They should show it in schools. It's an astonishingly good teaching tool – a way of showing children how life was for their grandparents and great-grandparents.' She's right. And if we show something terrible that's still happening today, those children might grow up and do something about it.

Thalidomide had been forgotten and we were able to remind audiences what happened, that there are victims who have never had proper compensation. It was the same when we did a story about homosexuality.

A lot of young crew members, around twenty-one or twenty-two, had no idea what we were doing – they couldn't quite comprehend. 'What do you mean it was illegal?' 'You could go to prison?' And the same again with abortion: the younger ones couldn't believe that it wasn't possible to get an abortion legally, that in many places you still can't, that women can die if they try and abort their own babies. *Call the Midwife* goes out in over two hundred territories all over the world, so it has a huge reach. We get thousands of letters and emails and social media posts. I remember a woman saying that she'd been living with her same-sex partner for forty years and had never felt able to tell anyone that they were a couple. She said that watching one of our episodes had released her and she felt that she could go out and talk about it. We talk to as many people as we possibly can to try to get it absolutely right – we do so much research. It's absolutely vital.

LEARNING THE LINES

Judy Parfitt

Sister Monica Joan

I do get some astonishingly ornate language, full of surprising constructs and syntax. It's unique to Sister Monica Joan. All the rest of the cast members say, 'I don't know how you learn it' – especially when Heidi gives me words that nobody uses any more. Sometimes it is quite difficult to remember them but it's a joy to deliver and just right for the character, with her particular combination of vulnerability and hauteur, mischief and spirituality.

Max Macmillan

Timothy Turner

I'm lucky to have a brain that's quite good at short-term memorising – lines of script, sheet music and stuff. Music and words help each other and sometimes when I'm trying to learn lines I give them a rhythm to help them settle or come more easily if they get caught up in your mouth. Now I have to use medical terms and it's a nightmare – working out how to pronounce eight-syllable words.

Jenny Agutter

Sister Julienne

I remember doing a scene with Bryony Hannah once, who was always very controlled and professional. It wasn't that I'd forgotten my lines but I had to come out with a medical word, something that I found completely unpronounceable. The shot was from behind me, over my shoulder, so I just made a sort of garbled sound – burbleburbleblometer. Bryony looked at me and she couldn't stop herself, she just fell apart laughing. It was lovely to see her completely go. Of course, I can remember what it was now; it was a blood-pressure measuring cuff – and I still can't say it. Sphygma – sphygmon – sphygmomanometer!

Linda Bassett

Phyllis Crane

At the start of filming a new series, we probably get an episode script a fortnight before shooting. Then, as things go on, it's maybe a week before, but then there are rewrites. We don't rehearse but we all know our characters extremely well and I work endlessly on learning my lines – Nurse Crane would be proud of me.

You need to know every word exactly, you'd trip over if you paraphrased, and spoil the cadence of the sentence. When I've got the script I work through it and through it, in story order. Then, as soon as I know the shooting schedule, I start relearning in shooting order so I'm not thrown by us chopping about. It's part of the job. It's fun.

THE MAGNIFICENT NURSE ON THE FLYING TRAPEZE

Linda Bassett

Phyllis Crane

An aspect of Phyllis that I like is her larky side – she'll suddenly kick over the traces a bit and race the girls up the stairs. What I did not expect was to be swinging on a trapeze dressed in a sequinned leotard! That Christmas episode was quite something, but you just have to go with these things. A bit like Nurse Crane, I couldn't resist the challenge!

Daniel Laurie

Reggie Jackson

The Christmas special with the circus and the big top was amazing. I got to work with a lot of new actors as well as some animals – the polar bear never turned up but there was a donkey! And I was very glad about Reggie getting to see Nurse Crane on the trapeze.

Jenny Agutter

Sister Julienne

I admire Linda Bassett so much as an actor and she's such a warm person – that Christmas episode was really startling and only Linda could have carried it off. The way she did it was to show that the child in her hadn't quite gone away – that child came out and was delighted. It was truly joyful.

THE POWER
OF MUSIC

Maurizio Malagnini

Composer, Series 4–10

There is a mixture of music on the show – music that I compose and music chosen from the period by the music supervisor. I am really happy when there's a great song that audiences will enjoy, that some of them will recognise. While the song is playing the story develops; you can sometimes cover three days of story in a song – it's a fantastic device of narration. I know that people can recognise musical themes – they've been hearing some of them for years now – and I like to manipulate them. So when Nurse Crane was on the trapeze in the Christmas special that melody, with rippling chords, comes originally from Series Six when we see a source of water – we see the water flowing. I thought, 'This is a very strong moment, an affirmation of life,' and I composed a crescendo to echo the swing of the trapeze. For an audience, there's no direct association, they're not aware it's there, but there's a subliminal connection and an emotional connection and that is something that keeps the show alive – along with the ability to stay creative and make things new.

There is humour also, and comedy. I find this more difficult to express with music but it's exactly what happens in normal life and Heidi is

incredibly good at capturing that swing. Even in the most difficult situations there is an element of comedy – through the eyes of the midwives, living their own lives, good days, bad days, love stories, moments of difficulty, of change. The development of the characters is what makes television work more interesting than work for the cinema. In a film, you sit down, you watch the film and after three hours it's finished – and usually you think that three hours is a bit too much! With television, in each episode, the characters undergo different experiences. Music can help portray a character's change. Sister Frances, for example – she's now more confident.

When the nuns sing in chapel – I consulted an expert in early music who helped train them for that – sometimes the scene is cut in a way so that we hear them singing and then we go into another scene and we hear the singing again. In that case, the singing is part of the narration. Diegetic is the term for sound that the characters can hear and extradiegetic is music that narrates the story. I can make very strong cues by using that device and changing from one to the other and the human voice enriches the palette of sound I can use. If I compose music to go over the singing of the nuns, it merges with the following cue and becomes something different from just singing – it expresses what is happening in the story.

It became a very powerful component of the music when Barbara died. There was a gospel choir singing 'Amazing Grace'. I worked on that with them. I gave them a backing track – they sang with freedom and spontaneity and I added some strings. It became diegetic because the character of Lucille was listening but also singing. It feels very close, bringing the audience into the same room because they're hearing the same thing as the characters for that moment. There is resonance and vibration and if they connect, the images take on another dimension. It's a sort of wizardry, a magical power.

SERIES TEN

1966

EPISODE ONE

Sister Julienne sends Trixie to work in the private Lady Emily Clinic to garner much needed funds for Nonnatus House, despite Dr Turner's strong objections. At the clinic, Trixie befriends new mother Fiona Aylward, while back in Poplar Cyril moves into the flat above the Buckles' paper shop with his church's financial support. Sister Monica Joan's crisis of faith continues to weigh heavily on her. Young couple Audrey and Derek Fleming are devastated when their baby boy is born with severely deformed limbs and dies soon after. The Nonnatuns fear the return of thalidomide but the child's death is revealed to be connected to Derek's military service during nuclear testing in the South Pacific.

EPISODE TWO

Married mum Jacinta O'Malley confesses that her new pregnancy is the result of an affair and plots a hasty adoption before seafaring husband Dessy gets home. When Dessy returns unexpectedly, Jacinta's secret is out and Sister Frances must navigate the complex family crisis. At the Lady Emily Clinic, Fiona Aylward is unexpectedly readmitted with advanced leukaemia after a collapse, while Trixie discovers that the clinic is performing illegal private abortions – forcing Sister Julienne to terminate the lucrative arrangement. Cyril, Fred and Violet help a family find shelter after being evicted from their home, while Fiona's death leaves Trixie greatly saddened and her loving husband Matthew a grieving new father.

EPISODE THREE

Sister Hilda and Dr Turner are baffled when a young woman presents with a complex range of worrying symptoms. The race is on to find a diagnosis for Louise Wrigley but Sister Hilda subsequently uncovers the psychological trauma at its heart. Elsewhere, Pat Williams, a mum of two, feels shamed by the threat her recent weight gain has placed on her forthcoming home birth until Lucille discovers an underlying medical cause. Cyril wants to treat Lucille to a special day out but his plans are confounded by her work. Sister Frances's toothache becomes something she can't avoid, while Shelagh takes a job overseeing pupil midwives at St Cuthbert's and formulates a plan to save Nonnatus House.

EPISODE FOUR

It's July 1966 and Britain is in the grip of World Cup fever. The nuns run a sweepstake, while Fred places a secret accumulator bet, which tests his patriotic loyalties. Back at Nonnatus House, four new pupil midwives make their entrance, with the friendly but impulsive Nancy Corrigan proving an instant handful. When seventeen-year-old Michael Leeks is hospitalised with an infected cyst, Nurse Crane and Dr Turner uncover the boy's secret life – but the parental shame it causes leads Michael to take drastic action. Trixie attends the christening for widower Matthew Aylward's son, while Cyril's impulsive music purchase upsets Lucille but leads to a change of heart and a romantic marriage proposal.

EPISODE FIVE

When bright teenager Jeanette falls pregnant by her boyfriend Glen, her over-protective mother Doris is determined to put the shameful

episode swiftly behind them with a discreet adoption, much to trainee Nancy's frustration. Elsewhere, Sister Julienne is concerned when pregnant Vera Sands' young daughter displays developmental problems; further investigation points to an undiagnosed genetic condition that threatens the new baby. Lucille and Cyril celebrate their engagement news with the community, while Trixie answers a parenting distress call from Matthew Aylward. Meanwhile, the Turners celebrate young Timothy's qualification for medical school.

EPISODE SIX

Sister Frances starts a maternity class for Asian mothers to ease cultural barriers. Raj Gupta wants pregnant wife Sarita to attend; her reluctance exposes a severe childhood trauma from Partition-era India. With Nonnatun support, Sarita eventually accepts help. Impoverished mum of four Cherry Watson is pregnant again by her violent husband and Dr Turner and Trixie diagnose an attempted self-abortion. Cherry's plight inspires Trixie to write to *The Times* regarding the need for abortion reform, which divides Nonnatus House and angers Nancy. Yet Trixie's subsequent impassioned radio appearance leads Nancy to confess the existence of her own secret child – a bombshell that places her in danger of expulsion.

EPISODE SEVEN

After Trixie and Sister Frances deliver a baby in a filthy tenement, Sister Frances demands that councillor Violet tackles the slum. When Matthew Aylward is revealed as the owner, Trixie encourages him to address his conscience and his grief. Forty-something mother Blanche is having her unplanned baby adopted by her sister Sylvia. When the child is born with Down's syndrome, Sylvia recoils. Blanche reclaims the boy, although her husband Walter needs the Buckles' help to adjust. Nancy visits her daughter at the orphanage but is angry at her treatment and runs away with her – compounding her problems until a compromise is found. Medical student Tim flies the Turner nest and Cyril and Lucille adjust their wedding plans.

BRINGING OUT THE BEST

Heidi Thomas

Writer and executive producer

There are little bits of me in a number of the characters. I wish I was as forthright as Sister Evangelina, as wise as Nurse Crane, as patient as Sister Julienne. Possibly the character most like me was Barbara. I gave her a Liverpool background, as I had. She was a vicar's daughter and I was a vicar's niece. If you took her at face value you wouldn't necessarily appreciate her – she was well-meaning and gauche and underestimated. I'm not sure why I identified with her so strongly but she'd gone through life being repeatedly pushed to one side and she was determined not to let that continue.

There is nothing whatever of myself in Trixie and I enjoy writing her all the more because of that. I wish I had her fashion sense! There are elements of my own experience in everything, though. Miss Higgins was named after my first primary school teacher, who taught me to read. The Turners' marriage definitely has something of my marriage but Stephen is not Patrick, although they share some characteristics. I adore Laura's characterisation of Shelagh – she's become so competent, and a bit of a fusspot.

Essentially, it's like writing for a repertory company. I know the actors' strengths and I like to think I can bring out the best in them, giving them material that will make them shine. Some people are naturally funny, like Charlotte Ritchie and Fenella Woolgar, who has the most brilliant comic timing. Ella Bruccoleri is funny in a completely different way – she has a comical sincerity. Helen George can deliver a long, reflective speech and has a lovely capacity to be nuanced and textured. Judy Parfitt is an absolute joy to write for – there is no elevation of the English language that she can't match. Daniel Laurie as Reggie is an extremely responsive actor. He listens to the other actors and has wonderful facial expressions so I make sure he has that opportunity and I script his unspoken responses. Jenny Agutter is one of the most poised and graceful women I've ever met – because she has such grace in her physical movements and in her emotional responses there is a very strong element of her in Sister Julienne.

I have worked very hard to represent the nuns' world fairly and to portray their spiritual as well as their practical life. A key point is that they are not liberal; they are compassionate and forgiving, which is completely different. It's been such a pleasure to write about people of faith in a way that doesn't poke fun at them, that respects their fundamental life choices. Jenny has no religious faith herself but finds a degree of fascination in Sister Julienne's spirituality. You have to believe that the nuns believe that they are called to this work – a life of prayer and a life of service. Their preoccupations are physical – blood and pain and excrement and suffering – but the beating pulse of the thing is their belief that they are in the right place, doing the right thing.

FILMING IN A TIME OF COVID

Annie Tricklebank

Producer, Series 4–10

I've started directing myself now, which is wonderful. Heidi and Pippa said to me one day, 'Why don't you do your own episode?' And I loved it – I love actors, working with them, talking to them. I wish I could have been one myself. I'm always offering to stand in for people and they say, 'You've got enough to do,' which is kind but frustrating! But I really enjoy the conversations. Actors will come to me with the script and want to talk through details. We discuss the dialogue and what it means. Then they say, 'Oh, yes, I see,' and they do the astonishing thing that never ceases to amaze me – they turn on a sixpence and become somebody else. How do they do that? I've tried and tried and I can't do it. I'm still me – I don't become somebody else.

There's so little time for the actors, it's incredibly pressured – they come in at 5.30 or 6 in the morning, shoot their scenes, go home and learn their lines for the next day. With Covid it's been even harder. We had people checking constantly that everyone was two metres apart and we had to devise the most complex ways of filming to try to make that look less extreme and somehow natural. With casting, we haven't been able to meet anyone in person so it's all been done on tape or Zoom.

Ella Bruccoleri

Sister Frances

I've never attended a birth or had a baby but I've always loved them and it was so sad not to be able to touch them in Series Ten because of Covid restrictions. Normally it's my favourite part – whenever a baby comes on set I can hold it in my arms between takes, have it breathing there. It calms me down. A film set can seem very chaotic, with everyone rushing around, focused on their own task. It's overwhelming sometimes. Terri Coates is very good at bringing things down. She does it for the baby's benefit but she's a soothing presence anyway. When you have a baby in your arms it takes you out of your own head; you stop worrying about unnecessary detail and your attention moves entirely onto this little creature. There's an acting exercise I remember doing at drama school where you do a speech pretending to care for a little bird at the same time – it's like that.

We didn't do any screen work at drama school and I feel very grateful that I've had so many days on a film set now, learning and watching. I think there are, in the simplest terms, two types of actor on film. The ones that tend to only give you something when the camera's on them and those who give it to you every time because they're in the moment. What's remarkable about this cast is that everyone is in the latter category. It's a testament to them, the casting director, the producers – and the writer. You might think that more experienced actors might be less generous but no, every single take they give you everything, every part of themselves. It's one of the most important things I've learnt – you have to give every time. It can be hard as sometimes you have to do the same thing upwards of twenty times, but it can be done. I'm so grateful for their generosity.

Judy Parfitt

Sister Monica Joan

I've been very grateful to be able to work but it's not been an easy time, mainly because we're like a family. After ten years, it's extraordinary that a core group of us are still together and over all that time we haven't had any rows or fallings out. We're supportive of each other, we hug each other, we care about each other and each other's families. To have to film with someone holding a tape measure and checking that you're always two metres away from anyone else has been pretty miserable. It made you feel isolated even when you were with others. And masks and wimples are a challenging combination. If you can't see another person's face properly it affects how you respond. It's why British actors are so good – they act *with* people, not *at* them; they know it has to be give and take, like tennis.

Filming at Nonnatus House was like acting in a freezer. I was wearing two lots of thermals and a mink coat that the actress Coral Browne left me – and clutching a hot-water bottle. We're social creatures and pack animals, and we need each other. At least I have my dog. He's a miniature poodle and a demanding one. He weighs one and a half kilos, he's nine inches long and recently he was walking around with a sprained leg – the front right one held up very high. I had to try not to laugh at him – he sometimes lost his balance and fell over when he tried to pee.

FIGHTING HER CORNER

Helen George

Trixie Franklin

Trixie has grown as a character and that makes her fascinating to play. She has a sensibility, an understanding of the female predicament that riles her and creates that passion to fight for women and for Nonnatus House. The 1960s were still very much a time when the rules were dictated by men and Trixie is fiercely determined not to be reverent towards men in suits in their fifties. In Series Ten, she writes a letter to *The Times* about the abortion bill because it's about to be debated in Parliament and gets invited onto BBC radio to talk about it, winding up at a table of white, middle-aged men who hardly let her get a word in edgeways. She eventually manages to chip in and is angry but highly articulate, talking about her first-hand experiences as a working mid-wife. We did the scene with this group of guys and they were really lovely but to my complete surprise it really shook me up. On set we usually have so few men – me as Helen freaked out a bit and I couldn't remember my lines. I had to work hard to regain my confidence.

When we started ten years ago, it was a major achievement for the producers to pitch successfully for a show with so many women, of varying ages – women in their twenties, forties, fifties and seventies as

central characters, with no big male names in the cast. It was genuinely brave and ahead of its time, and not glamorous either, in a glossy Hollywood way. Nuns and midwives not wearing any make-up, no cheating and applying a sneaky bit of blusher. And the world of the East End at the beginning was desperately poor. You know it would have smelt really bad, too – an assault on the senses. When I was growing up, my mum used to take us to visit her family in York and we'd go to the JORVIK Viking Centre where they have a trail with an awful stench. I used to try to summon that up. The tenement buildings that were still standing after the Blitz were squalid and damp and had bugs in the walls, and that went on into the 1960s.

NO FILTER

Megan Cusack

Nancy Corrigan

I had a character description – I knew that Nancy was an orphan and that she'd been brought up by nuns – and I had the script for the first episode, but I didn't know what the trajectory of her story might turn out to be. She was good fun, a bit wild and outspoken, she had no filter, and from the start she was always running because she was late, or about to be. Then it turned out that she had this horrific backstory. In the second episode there's a young mother who ends up giving up her baby for adoption, and Nancy says, 'It's an awful hard decision to give a baby up.' I remember reading that in the script and thinking, 'Hmm, I feel like there's something there' – I'm very astute! – and so I texted Annie Tricklebank to ask her to give me a bit of a lead so I'd know how to play that line, whether to give it a bit of emphasis, and she told me that Nancy had got pregnant and had a baby when she was very young. What I didn't know until later was that she'd been subjected to some really tough treatment and that her daughter, Collette, who's been placed in an orphanage in London, was at risk from the same sort of thing. It was such a shock to discover that.

Francesca Fullilove, who plays Collette, is an absolute delight. The first scene we had together was when Nancy – who Collette thinks is her sister – goes to visit. We were sitting there in between takes and

Francesca goes, 'I don't think I got that first line quite right – I think I should be more excited to see you,' and I said, 'That's OK, we'll be doing it again.' We had another go and she said, 'Yes, that felt much better. I got it that time.' She's brilliantly professional, does the job properly. Someone asked her if she wanted to be an actress when she was older and she said, 'Oh no, I want to be a post lady.' Clever girl, I thought, none of this risky acting stuff, get the job done nice and early and have the rest of the day to yourself!

Nancy's only twenty-one and she's a fighter, she's passionate and determined, which lands her in trouble. If you haven't had anyone helping you in life, you feel as if it's only you – you've got to do everything for yourself. It doesn't occur to her to ask anyone for help. I must say, wondering what she might have been through has kept me up at night, but I've decided that it was probably what must have happened to a lot of girls in Ireland – because there was no sexual education what-ever, a lot of them quite literally didn't know what sex was. They were taught that you could only have babies when you were married, but they didn't have any idea what that involved and getting pregnant came as a complete shock. It's a hard thing to get your head wrapped around, that it really wasn't that long ago – it was happening to people of my parents' age. I loved it when Nancy goes off to rescue Collette and nobody knows where she's gone. Sister Monica Joan says that she must have gone to find her child, but nobody listens to her. She's right of course, so the moral of that is, ALWAYS LISTEN TO SISTER MONICA JOAN!

It's great that Nancy wears some really bonkers clothes. And she breaks the unspoken rules of Nonnatus House without realising she's doing it. She sits on the arms of chairs! She puts her elbows on the table when she's eating! Jenny Agutter was horrified – she said, 'I think Sister Julienne will have to have words with you about that.'

NEW BOY ON THE BLOCK

Olly Rix

Matthew Aylward

I've been lucky enough to be working pretty much non-stop for the past few years and I haven't been watching much television, so although I knew about *Call the Midwife* and its popularity, and had seen a few episodes, I was blissfully unaware of quite how huge that popularity was. Rather naively I remember saying to a few American and Australian friends that I was going into this BBC drama, but they probably wouldn't have seen it. When I mentioned the title, of course they knew all about it and had been watching since Series One!

Matthew is an interesting character to play because he's so privileged by his wealthy background but constrained and hemmed in by it as well. He's very happy with his wife Fiona and the birth of their son – they have a warm and loving relationship – but he does things the way he's expected to do them, staying outside the delivery room at the private clinic, for example, until he realises that it's possible to do things differently. Trixie gives him permission, in a way, to be a father, to make his own decisions. When Fiona dies unexpectedly, he's not just grieving, he's dealing with a newborn child and a drastically changed way of living. What I did become increasingly aware of, along with the size

of the audience, was how loyal viewers are, and how protective of much-loved characters. If I, as Matthew, had done anything to diminish or 'save' Trixie in any way, there'd have been big trouble. Fortunately, the writing doesn't allow that for an instant – people did pick up on an onscreen chemistry but when Matthew first appeared he was a married man with a pregnant wife and absolutely nothing inappropriate was going to happen. Trixie is the one who takes the lead as far as practical help is concerned and putting him on the right tracks. The storyline of Matthew turning out to be a slum landlord was completely unexpected. Trixie is quite rightly enraged by the filth and overcrowding she finds in the buildings that Matthew turns out to own and, to give him his due, once she shows him what appalling conditions his tenants are living in, he faces up to that and sets out to put things right. There's an unwavering moral compass on *Call the Midwife* and most of the characters in it are genuinely good people, trying to do their best. Matthew wants to help, and to do something in memory of his dead wife – he doesn't just swoop in and think he can solve everything by writing a cheque. Although Sister Julienne is extremely grateful when he does that!

Heidi's way of writing informs everything about the show – it's fascinating to me that what's on the page doesn't come naturally, because it's deliberately constructed as a period piece. My natural instinct is to be very throwaway, to act 'off the line', but that wouldn't work here. Matthew speaks in a heightened manner, quite considered and clipped, and the script dictates that, it directs you in that way – the writing does the work for you. And I also like the way that the costumes reflect his situation – he's even hemmed in by his own clothes; all those three-piece suits with buttoned-up waistcoats, it's like a form of armour.

DECADE OF CHANGE

Julia Castle

Production designer, Series 8–10

The world of Nonnatus House, with its long corridor and dark brown polished wood, has remained the same visually because there would never have been any spare money to spend on it, but other things have changed as time has gone on. The maternity home is greener and fresher, with cleaner colours, and the Lady Emily private clinic in Series Ten is thoroughly up-to-date with modern art on the walls.

Maintenance of the sets is quite hard because they were originally built to last for three years and we're now seven years beyond that. We titivate all the time and recently we've done a big repair job on them to make sure they're safe. When I get a script I'll work out which rooms I can use and what needs to be changed. We're constantly rebuilding and we have three or four of what are known as 'turnaround sets', which are the same basic structure but redecorated, reconfigured, doors moved. Most of the doors only have a minimal space behind them and we put up a bit of wallpaper to make it look as if the room keeps going behind what can be seen on screen. None of the houses are full scale but they look as if they are – and in some cases we only ever film through the windows, to give an impression of an interior. Violet's haberdashery is like an extension of her own personality and rather than change it dramatically, which she wouldn't have done, we've just started putting in rolls of more modern fabrics and 1960s paper patterns. My dad had a cycle shop, which his grandfather had before him, and it basically stayed the same for years – it was just the things in it that changed.

IT GOES ON

Stephen McGann

Dr Turner

'You're . . . joking . . .?!'

Heidi stirs slowly, her eyes barely able to open. It's early on Monday, 19 April 2021. The bedroom is still dark as she's sleeping off another night of writing till dawn. I'm waking her with good news. Last night's viewing figure for the first episode of *Call the Midwife*'s tenth series was a whopper. Again. After ten years.

I hear Heidi take a deep breath, letting the tension go from her body. She smiles, eyes still closed. 'It goes on, Judah, it goes on,' she says.

The remark is our private joke – a reference to the famous chariot-and-sandals epic *Ben-Hur*. The chief Roman villain Messala croaks this line to Charlton Heston on his death bed, to indicate that their private battle – and Ben-Hur's personal labours – will go on, despite Messala's demise.

The previous week, the BBC had been in touch to recommission *Call the Midwife* for another two series, taking the drama all the way to 1969: an incredible thirteen-year run. And now our audience had demonstrated, again, their love and support for the show, by watching the opening episode of Series Ten in huge numbers.

I knew what Heidi meant. The feeling wasn't one of triumph. It was a feeling of immense gratitude mixed with relief and a renewed sense of obligation. Series Ten had taken place under the extraordinarily trying circumstances of a deadly pandemic. But we'd somehow done it. Now there was no time for slacking. Our audience deserves no less. It goes on.

Series Nine had begun screening in January 2020 with an outbreak of diphtheria that the Poplar community had been desperate to trace and eradicate before innocent lives were lost. But nobody knew then that within weeks of the episode being broadcast a much more deadly infection crisis would strike Britain and suspend all plans for filming Series Ten. It was life upstaging drama in the most sombre fashion.

Like everybody else in the country, we sat at home, isolated and uncertain. Yet we were determined to resume our work under whatever restrictions were necessary to do it safely. It was autumn before we finally got the call to return to the set. We now had to film through the winter of 2020 and into 2021 to catch up – something we'd never had to do before. Instead of complaining about being too hot in warm clothing while filming Christmas in a heatwave, our actors could now complain about shivering in summer clothing! The studios couldn't be heated in the usual way as our heaters blew hot air – a distinct Covid hazard. So we were now forced to experience the post-war joys of seeing our own breath inside the buildings in which we worked.

There were many important restrictions placed on our production in order for filming to continue – most related to wearing masks and keeping adequate distance from each other to prevent spread. This presented immediate challenges. Drama is essentially a contact sport. It exists to show human interaction – and none more so than a medical drama, which is literally about medics placing healing hands on others. But the screen industry is also a problem-solving machine. Every day on set, even in healthy times, there are a million tiny problems to address: bad weather, power failure, lost light, delays, script changes, aircraft noise, actor illness, camera faults, etc., etc. We're used to tackling what's in front of us and finding solutions. It was the same with Covid-19. As we began to film, we stopped complaining and worked together to achieve the scenes we needed, despite the restrictions we faced. We are a

close-knit production but there was an added camaraderie about the way we went about it, director and crew collaborating with the cast to work around specific technical challenges. We worked it out. Together.

At the heart of this collective action was genuine humility. We were the lucky ones and we knew it. We were simply actors, not the real medics. Our tiny problems were trivial next to the heroics of the real-life nurses and doctors battling the virus in Britain's hospitals. Many had already died doing their jobs. Covid-19 wasn't an inconvenience to them; it was life and death. Our job was to give people locked down at home something meaningful to watch. And, hopefully, an assurance that certain aspects of their society could continue despite the crisis.

Society. Such a small word. But one that carries with it such immense gravity. From the beginning, *Call the Midwife* has been focused on a central lesson regarding post-war British health that was suddenly thrust back into the limelight with the Covid-19 pandemic. The formation of the National Health Service after the war had ushered in an era of 'big health', which – along with the miracle of antibiotics, new vaccines and mass testing – offered society the chance to eradicate infectious evils that had plagued it for centuries: polio, measles, small-pox, diphtheria, tuberculosis. But to do it, society had to work with the NHS to tackle these enemies together. All as one. Mass vaccination. Mass testing. Rooting out infection and killing it as a whole community, not as individuals. Infectious disease doesn't care about your personal choices or opinions; it'll kill you just the same if it gets the chance. But if you all work together, you can beat it.

This was the priceless wisdom of post-war medicine. The one that had finally beaten those ancient diseases. Community and collective action are ultimately necessary for our survival on the planet. When crisis strikes, we all need each other to think of each other. Society is essential for life.

Call the Midwife has dramatised the importance of community and collective compassion for ten whole years. Time and again, we have shown the hard-learnt lessons of post-war medicine. Together we thrive. Alone and divided we die. For years, our show had been dismissed by some as being 'cosy', or 'escapist', or 'soft-centred'. Yet in 2020, we could see the appalling result of nations, societies or communities that failed to act collectively in the face of a new deadly disease, and the fate of those individuals who indulged in personal freedoms or wants at the expense of others' lives. There was nothing 'soft' or 'cosy' about the deaths that resulted from a failure to remember the past or the importance of society.

So there is, I think, something moving and appropriate about the tenth-anniversary series of *Call the Midwife* taking place under the sober shadow of a National Health Service mobilised to heroic community action in the face of danger. It's a reminder that the central message of Nonnatus House is as important now as it has ever been. We all got from there to here because we cared enough about each other to make miracles as one. There will be more diseases to come in our world. More danger to threaten us. But if we all care enough about each other, and about our collective dignity, then there is nothing we cannot heal. That is *Call the Midwife* in a nutshell.

So happy tenth anniversary to my precious drama. My modest, brave, gentle, strong, important, loving, caring *Call the Midwife*. For wearing its lessons so lightly. But for bringing to millions a reminder of the lessons we must never allow ourselves to forget.

And the future?

It goes on, Judah. It goes on!

ACKNOWLEDGEMENTS

A TV production is the work of hundreds of creative minds and skills, most of them labouring unseen. To acknowledge every individual who has paddled away in the weeds over the past ten years to make *Call the Midwife* the elegant swan it is would take an entire book in itself. My deepest thanks to every one of you; to the directors, the writers, the editors, the production designers, assistant directors, costume teams, make-up staff, post-production teams, catering crews, the production office, the accountants, script editors, casting directors, camera teams, sound departments, transport staff, gaffers, set builders, props handlers, music department, researchers, location finders, photographers, series publicists, medics, and everybody at Neal Street Productions and the BBC, who work so hard to ensure we still have a pond to paddle in every year.

Special thanks to Annie Tricklebank, Pippa Harris and Heidi Thomas – the greatest executive team in the business; to my agent Annabel Merullo and to Maddy Price, Georgia Goodall and everyone at Weidenfeld & Nicolson for making this book a reality; to Caroline Reynolds, who has paddled more than most; to Michael Earl, my driver and my friend; and to Stella O'Farrell, for her infinite patience and perfect scissors.

Finally, my greatest thanks to my partner in crime, the brilliant Henrietta Bredin, for her intelligence, her timely insights, her skilful interlocution, her infectious good humour and her superb eye.